Best Foot Forward

Life lessons from the world of dance

SHIRLEY
BALLAS

BOOKS

BBC BOOKS

UK | USA | Canada | Ireland | Australia
India | New Zealand | South Africa

BBC Books is part of the Penguin Random House group of companies whose
addresses can be found at global.penguinrandomhouse.com

Penguin Random House UK
One Embassy Gardens, 8 Viaduct Gardens, London SW11 7BW

penguin.co.uk
global.penguinrandomhouse.com

| Penguin
Random House
UK

First published by BBC Books in 2025

1

Typeset by seagulls.net
Printed and bound in Great Britain by Clays Ltd, Elcograf S.p.A.

The authorised representative in the EEA is Penguin Random House Ireland,
Morrison Chambers, 32 Nassau Street, Dublin D02 YH68.

A CIP catalogue record for this book is available from the British Library

ISBN 9781785949784

Penguin Random House is committed to a sustainable future
for our business, our readers and our planet. This book is
made from Forest Stewardship Council® certified paper.

Best Foot Forward

ALSO BY SHIRLEY BALLAS

Behind the Sequins

To everyone who has supported me in the eight years
since I started on Strictly Come Dancing.
Your positivity, messages and friendship
have meant the absolute world.
From the bottom of my heart, thank you.

CONTENTS

Introduction

I always assumed that by the time I reached my sixties I'd have everything figured out. Thanks to a wealth of experience gathered from the decades of twists and turns, I'd be like a wise old owl with the meaning of life completely cracked.

Hey, no laughing at the back.

But here I am, knocking on the door of 65 and only now realising that I'm never going to come close to having all the answers. Just when you think you've nailed the routine, along comes a giant glitter ball to knock you off your feet again.

What I *do* know is that each one of those setbacks has shaped me into the person I am today – every kick in the teeth has something to teach us if we're willing to listen.

And that's what this book is all about.

When I wrote my bestselling autobiography *Behind the Sequins* five years ago, telling my story in full for the first time, I felt that I'd finally found my voice. From the years growing up stony broke, to conquering the world of dance, from the divorces, heartbreaks, betrayals and grief all the way through to landing the job of a lifetime on *Strictly Come Dancing*, being able to write my truth and share some of the pain I've carried was incredibly liberating.

I know many of you will have read it and the outpouring of love and positive feedback from fans and followers – my team – was phenomenal.

Best Foot Forward is the companion to that memoir, an opportunity to look a little closer at the struggles, the triumphs and the drive which pushes me on every step of the way.

I want to draw on everything I've been through to show that hope can rise from despair, it's never too late to make a change and that even when the music stops, you can find your sparkle again.

In many ways I feel very fortunate. I have friends and family who love me and the sort of career that dreams are made of. I could never have imagined where it would take me when I first set foot on a ballroom floor at the age of just seven.

But nothing was ever handed to me on a silver platter – everything I have and own, I've worked hard for, which is why I cherish it with all my being.

And despite all the many good things in my life, I've also suffered a hell of a lot of bad luck along the way and survived more than my fair share of heartache.

I lost my brother to suicide, a grief which is still raw more than 20 years later.

I've loved ferociously and given everything to those relationships, but have had my heart shattered and been left with nothing.

I've lived in luxury, but I've also been on the bones of my arse and had to start over again from scratch several times.

And throughout all of that, I like to think I've stayed true to who I am. My core values have remained steadfast; they are foundations which have kept me grounded, whatever storms I've had to weather.

The backbone to all of this has been the discipline instilled in me from childhood, nearly all of which I attribute to dance.

Right from the beginning, dance came first and I knew what it meant to be committed.

At home, I was given the gift of resilience by my formidable mother who worked multiple jobs while my brother and I managed the household, learning to cook a Sunday roast between us before the age of ten. That was our reality.

The discipline fed the resilience and the resilience fed the discipline. Each reinforced the other.

You're going to get to know my mother, Audrey, very well throughout the course of this book. Along with my son, she is the most important relationship in my life – she is stoicism personified, my leading light and number-one confidante.

It's for that reason that I've started each of my chapters – which I'm calling 'steps' – with a quote from her, a golden nugget of no-nonsense advice, every word of which has served me well over the years.

You'll also see I've signed off each step with a bunch of Shirley's Shimmers, a collection of final thoughts which I hope you'll take heart from.

Over the next few hundred pages, I'm going to revisit some of the experiences you might remember from *Behind the Sequins* as well as opening up about many others I've not felt ready to share until now. And of course, there are five more years to catch up on since I wrote it and if you know anything about me by now it's that I can pack an awful lot into a short space of time.

I've had a cancer scare, seen the stalker who terrorised me for six years brought to justice and I find myself single again, wondering if I'll ever find lasting love. I've judged five more series of *Strictly*, fought my way through Bear Grylls's jungle and also become a grandmother to the most gorgeous baby boy, Banksi Wylde Ballas, who has given me a whole new perspective on the world.

Heartache, mental health, loneliness, menopause, bunions and plenty more besides – my hope is that by sharing the warts and all, you might at least find some reassurance that you're not alone in navigating the footwork of life.

Perhaps together, we can make sense of the steps.

Maybe life is supposed to be one huge learning curve from the day we're born until the day we bow out for good. Maybe we're never meant to know it all.

Just before we begin, I'd like to take a moment to thank you all for being here. Not just for this book, but for everything, the whole shebang.

I really do have a wonderfully loyal community out there who support me through thick and thin. Having you here is like falling into a cloud; you're always cushioning me and you constantly have my back on this wildest of rides which shows no signs of slowing down.

I've no intention of allowing it to. I will never stand still.

I want to keep learning, keep growing and keep dancing, right until the very end, until I click my clogs.

So, let me take you by the hand and lead you to the dance floor for the whirl and twirl of a lifetime.

STEP ONE

Put Your Best Foot Forward

AMBITION

'Just get to the front of the queue, Shirley.'

AUDREY

*L*ife, much like dance, is all about movement. Every step you take can shape the direction in which you're heading and putting your best foot forward means showing up with intention, playing to your strengths and having a willingness to work hard.

Not to mention a point-blank refusal ever to throw the towel in.

Someone once said to me, 'It doesn't matter how we try to push you down, Shirley Ballas, you just keep on resurfacing.' Now, you might think that was meant as an insult, and knowing who the remark came from, it probably was. At least in part.

But I have always taken it as the highest compliment because it gets right to the heart of who I am. No matter how many times life has tried to knock me down or throw me off course, I've always found a way to get up, dust myself off and come back again, even stronger than before.

It's a never-say-die attitude that I get from my mother and I've needed every bit of it to survive nearly 60 years in a dance industry that is not for the faint-hearted.

It's a tough, unforgiving, deeply flawed and dog-eat-dog world. It's where my passion, my perseverance and purpose have been tested – and indeed proven – time and time again.

But despite all its imperfections, it is where I belong.

It's what I know and what I am best at, and despite the often-relentless bullying, backstabbing and betrayals, my dedication to it has never wavered.

Even now, if I'm asked to do something for my industry, I always try my utmost to fulfil that request and give back. I love it with every fibre of my soul and I will die in my dance shoes.

I know many people spend a lifetime searching for their dream, but I was lucky enough to stumble across mine at the age of seven. My mother always encouraged me to give anything I fancied a go, which is why at various points in my early childhood she had me trying out tennis, chess, tap, ballet, swimming, volunteering for the Red Cross and singing in the choir.

I guess a scattergun approach to activities is one way of figuring out where your strengths lie – what sparks joy and what makes you tick.

My epiphany came on an otherwise ordinary evening at Brownies in my local church hall. We were learning how to perform CPR when the faint sound of music coming from one of the adjoining rooms caught my attention.

And in that moment, everything – the whole course of my life – changed forever.

I was immediately drawn to the sound and found myself walking towards it. It was almost hypnotic and I felt a rush of energy surge through my body as I moved closer.

I peered through the glass at the top of the door and saw people moving to music. There was, elegance, connection and magic … I was mesmerised.

It took my breath away.

A gentleman in the room spotted me watching and asked if he could help me.

'What are they doing?' I asked him.

He told me they were learning the Waltz. And, as luck would have it, they were starting children's classes that very Saturday. That's serendipity right there, isn't it?

Just like that, I'd found my calling, a passion which has shaped my whole life and taken me on the most exhilarating of journeys, all the way to head judge on *Strictly Come Dancing*.

But before we get into all of that, I'd like to rewind a little and take you back to the very beginning, to give you the back-drop which puts into context everything that has unfolded in my life since.

I was born Shirley Annette Rich on 6 September 1960 in Highfield Hospital in Wallasey and spent the first couple of years of my life living in my great-grandfather's house in New Brighton, a seaside resort and suburb of Wallasey in the Wirral, along with my maternal grandparents Frank and Daisy, my mother Audrey and older brother David.

My dad, George Andrew Rich (who was known as Andy) was largely absent, having left when I was two and David was three and a half – he and my mother had a volatile relationship with explosive arguments fuelled by his drinking.

While he would visit occasionally, he never gave us a red cent. I remember my mum taking him to court where he was ordered to pay a small amount to support us, but we didn't ever receive it. Off he went and lived his life, marrying three more times after my mother divorced him. Our father–daughter relationship was often so distant that it was easier to call him Andy than Dad or Daddy.

Although years later I was told by other people that he was proud of me, actions speak much louder than words as far as I'm concerned. It's all well and good saying, 'Oh, I love my daughter because she's on the telly' but that's not what love is to me.

When people go out on a limb for you, that's when you know you've got a good person in your corner. My father never did that.

Not that I've ever blamed him for anything that's gone wrong in my life – I only ever take responsibility for that myself – but I still hold some anger that he didn't have it in him to step up to the plate when we needed him.

I'm mad at him because of the way I know he treated my mother. I'm mad about the fact he never took responsibility and then told other people that *we* were the issue, not him. I'm mad that he never actually sat down and said, 'You know what, Shirley, I wasn't the world's greatest dad, please let me try to make it up to you.'

My mother never married again and I think he put her through a lot more than perhaps she cares to share – although by the time she got her divorce, her heart hadn't just healed, it was singing.

Not long after my father walked out on us, she was offered a council flat three miles along the coast on the Leasowe housing estate, a tight-knit community where it was common for generations of the same families to live on neighbouring streets.

We hardly had two pennies to rub together and I spent large parts of my childhood fending for myself because my mother was always out working multiple jobs, trying to earn enough to keep our heads above water. But I never felt hard done by and am forever proud of those working-class roots.

I refused to allow being 'a kid from a housing estate' to hold me back. In fact, it would turn out to be one of my greatest strengths, not least because there have been countless occasions when I've been able to surprise those who underestimated me.

Although other people I've come across in the dance industry and the wider world have been born into privilege and had easier access to opportunities, I had determination, guts, resourcefulness and a hunger to push beyond expectations.

Where you start out doesn't have to put a limit on where you can go.

I was picked on for being in receipt of free meals but that didn't bother me. It was different for my brother David; he would just about die of shame if he had to stand in the free lunch queue, whereas I was more pragmatic and just saw it as a way of getting a good hot dinner in my belly as opposed to a soggy butty.

On the Leasowe, we lived at number 61 Cameron Road on the second floor of the block in a two-bedroom flat which my mother kept spotless. We had no fridge, no phone or washing machine, but we did have a coal fire and Mum made that place a beautiful home. On top of working relentlessly, she ensured it was spick and span.

She'd risk life and limb to clean the windows – I can still picture her now, clear as day, as I was coming home from school.

'Is that your mother hanging from the window at the top?' asked my friends, shocked and impressed in equal measure.

It sure was, God love her.

Later, we moved opposite, to number 43, which was an upgrade – a marvellous little three-bed house that had its own yard – but we always lived very much hand to mouth and David and I were expected to muck in with the shopping and cooking, keeping the plates spinning while Mum was at work.

Despite the various hardships we had to contend with, I remember it as a carefree life in many ways. My friends and I would play out on the street with our marbles – 'ollies' as we used to call them on Merseyside – and we'd spend the weekends at the Derby Pool in Wallasey, a huge lido which has sadly long since shut down.

My mum always did the best she could in extremely tough circumstances. She's an indomitable woman, always smiling, never grumbling. She could be as sick as a dog, but you wouldn't ever hear that woman complain.

'We don't do moaning in this house,' she'd say.

Still says that.

Because I knew she struggled to provide everything, I took great care of what few possessions I had. I remember one day we went into Marks & Spencer where she spotted a beautiful dark brown velvet jacket for me. Velvet was very popular at the time, but Marksies was too expensive for us, so she found a cheaper version in Littlewoods next door.

When we got home, she stewed over it because she always wanted me to have the best and, in the end, she returned the less expensive jacket and managed to cobble together the funds to buy the lovelier one from M&S after all.

So, I was never the child who mislaid a jumper or scuffed my shoes and I'm like that to this day – I crave consistency, organisation and need to know where everything is. I value everything I own and rarely lose anything.

I was a very instinctive child, vigilant and quick on the uptake – you don't get those skills by being spoiled rotten. You get them because you have to learn to survive.

'You will recognise your own path when you come upon it, because you will suddenly have all the energy and imagination you will ever need.'

JERRY GILLIES

There's a little poetic expression I love and which I use a lot when teaching.

'Devotion to the motion equals emotion.'

The more you devote to your craft and the more you can move your body, the greater the emotion you'll feel and convey. The reason I like it so much is because it doesn't just apply to dance – in a broader sense it's about the relationship between effort and outcome and how pouring your heart and soul into something can fuel a fire.

That's exactly what I did from the moment I began my ballroom journey following that chance encounter at Brownies. It meant I had to give up the ballet lessons I'd been attending since I was two because we didn't have the money for me to do both, so the pursuit of one dream meant the end of something else.

But that's just the way it was. When you're working just to scrape by, as my mother always was, you have to make tough choices – although there were a few things she refused to compromise on and that was putting good food on the table and a decent pair of shoes on our feet.

Knowing that we'd both made sacrifices for me to go along to ballroom classes gave me an extra bite. I never once took those lessons for granted. I wouldn't say I was the most talented dancer by any stretch of the imagination, but I was definitely the one who never missed a class. I was devoted to the art of dance.

Without fail, I went along every Saturday to Vic and May Knox's studio in the church hall and grafted like a demon to pick the steps up quickly – I wasn't born with a natural dancing ability, but I knew how to plug away and persist. I firmly believe that you don't have to be the most skilful or accomplished in your field, whatever it is, to make it to the top. It's not the fanciest footwork but the determination to get up, show up and outwork everyone else which will set you apart.

Talent will get you so far. It's hard work which really takes you places.

Not even the setbacks (and there were many) could shake my resolve. Every three months at Vic and May's, we'd undergo these medal tests followed by an open evening where all the kids could showcase their talents to family and friends. There was a big silver trophy up for grabs that night, but I never won it. I'd often get highly commended and always got the highest marks, but I wasn't ever quite 'good' enough … I felt that injustice so keenly.

However, rather than dampen my spirits, I think it lit a flame in me. Giving up would have been the easy option, but I wanted that silver trophy and every time I was snubbed, it spurred me on. Those kinds of knockbacks tend to have that effect on me. Over the years, I've lost count of the number of times I've been told I'd never amount to anything, but whenever somebody has said 'you can't', it's made me grit my teeth, dig my heels in and try again.

And powering this determination was the fact I'd fallen hook, line and sinker for dance. It was like stepping into another world, one which was extraordinary to me. The music, the expression, the way every movement told a story, it made my heart race, and it felt like home.

At the Knoxes' studio I'd been paired with another little girl called Irene Hamilton who was a neighbour on the Leasowe housing estate, although her family were well off compared to us. The Hamiltons had a car, which was vital once we started to compete, and they were happy to drive the two of us to various competitions around Wales and the Northwest.

However, there was a sinister side to life in that dance studio. Put it this way, things went on with regard to other girls which absolutely shouldn't have and when I told my mum about them, she pulled me out of there immediately. Irene's mother got her out too and they moved us both to Margaret Redmond's over the River Mersey in Crosby. It was 13 miles away but Irene's dad drove us there and back.

Margaret was a renowned Latin teacher – her father Alf taught ballroom while her mother, Florence, made all the dresses and boy oh boy were they the best in the business – and both Irene and I came on leaps and bounds under her tutelage. So the decision to move, although forced by other events, turned out to be game-changing. I sometimes look back at it as a *Sliding Doors* moment, a tweak that triggered a domino effect and changed everything.

Not long after we left the Knox studio, Irene and I won a silver trophy at the Capitol Ballroom in Liscard and I've still got it to this day. It's only small, but that trophy was symbolic of something bigger.

Irene and I had been at Margaret's for a few months when she floated the idea of pairing us up with boy partners – two she knew well had become available, one of them being a boy called David Fleet who was already very experienced and super talented.

The Hamiltons were certain that Irene was going to nab David because they had the finances to support the partnership, plus the car to get them to and from competitions. But after both of us had danced with him, Margaret announced, 'David would like to dance with Shirley.'

I was gobsmacked. It was the first moment I'd ever felt worthy of anything and I'll never forget that. But David's decision to choose me caused an uproar and even though Irene lived just a few roads away, her father never drove me to Crosby again. Now, you might think this was ridiculously petty of them. And you'd be right! But it wasn't a situation I spent a single minute getting in a flap about – that wasn't how my mother had raised me. It was merely the latest obstacle in my life that I had to find a solution for.

I worked out that to get myself to Margaret's Crown Studios, I'd have to walk from my house to the bus stop, hop on the bus to Leasowe train station, catch the train to Liverpool Central, run across the city to the old Ribble bus station and then jump on the Ribble bus to Crosby.

It was about two hours door-to-door and I made that journey every single week from the age of 12.

The mind boggles now with all the potential dangers for a young girl venturing across towns and cities on her own, but at the time it was a case of needs must and the only possible way I could continue with the thing I loved most.

As winter drew in and the nights started getting darker, my mother arranged for me to stay with David's family from the Friday night to the Sunday night. We'd practise when I arrived at his, have our lesson with Margaret on the Saturday and then I'd make my way back on the Sunday evening, running across Liverpool to catch the train in the pitch black with sweat pouring down my back.

I'd get off at Hoylake, which is where my mother worked in Finnigan's steakhouse, and I started waiting tables there, working late before coming home with Mum in the early hours.

It didn't take me long to work out that you got good tips from the customers if you went the extra mile, so I injected a bit of personality into my waitressing spiel.

'Hands up if you want the pie! Hands up if you want the steak!' I'd call out rather than meekly taking down their orders, and they liked that bit of feistiness. It made me stand out. You were supposed to put your tips in a jar to be shared among all the staff, but I knew I worked harder than everybody else, so I used to stick mine straight down my little padded bra.

When I got home, I'd unclip the bra and all the coins would clatter to the floor. I'd stack them up on the telly and say to my mum, 'Put that towards the shoes,' knowing how much she scrimped and saved to afford the gear I needed for dance.

David Fleet and I were often competing on the Sunday and although Margaret Redmond would drive us there from the studio, I had to get myself home to Wallasey from any number of different locations across the region. I got used to asking people for help. My mother always said I had no shame, but I don't think it was that – it was born out of necessity. Dance felt like my destiny and I had to find whichever way I could to make this work.

I'd got to know some of the older couples on the competition circuit – Zoe and Charles were one, Frank and Lil another – and if I spotted them at the venue we were competing in, I knew I'd have a ride home and could rest easy that I was getting back safely that evening.

Their kindness has stayed with me and is one of the reasons I always make sure I go through life paying it forward. Generosity should have a ripple effect. If someone is good to us, we have a responsibility to find a way of giving back to somebody else who hasn't had it quite as breezy.

My mother was always working but she made time to watch me dance whenever she could. Every month she'd come along with her best friend, my auntie Mavis, to the competition at the Capitol Ballroom, and once I started going to the iconic Blackpool Tower Ballroom – the undisputed home of ballroom dancing – she'd make sure her bum was on that front-row seat watching her little girl dance. But the regular here, there and everywhere competitions, she simply wasn't able to attend.

This was all perfectly normal to me; I didn't know any different and I'm so grateful when I look back because without those skills, I wouldn't have been so self-sufficient my whole life.

I was learning how to manoeuvre, how to survive and go it alone.

It was sink or swim.

> '*Passion is energy.*
> *Feel the power from focusing*
> *on what excites you.*'
>
> OPRAH WINFREY

There comes a point when chasing the dream means taking it to the next level. And knowing when to make that move up the gears is key.

Although David Fleet and I did quite well together for a while – semi-finalists in the junior Latin championships and fourth place in the north of England junior ballroom finals – the partnership was never destined for greatness.

So when I was offered the opportunity for a try-out with ex-junior British ballroom champion Nigel Tiffany, I didn't hesitate. When we arrived, Nigel actually thought he was trying out with my mother – that's how young and gorgeous she was!

Nigel was 18 and four years older than me and dancing with him would be a huge step up the ladder – indeed, my mother initially put her foot down and said absolutely not because she couldn't afford either the lessons we'd need or the travel costs for competitions.

Nevertheless, I was encouraged to give it a go by my good friend Neil Lunt, who came from a famous Liverpool dancing family, and as soon as Nigel took me in his arms, I was sold.

You could say that I was swept off my feet.

My mother always managed to find it in the budget to stretch to one private lesson a week, but the finances were the least of my worries. Nigel lived nearly 80 miles away in Shipley, West Yorkshire, which gave me my biggest transport headache to date. Getting there involved a bus, three trains and hours of travelling – each way – which simply wasn't sustainable every weekend.

In the end, dancing with Nigel meant moving to Shipley, which was a big decision for my mother and a huge wrench for me. I was still only 14, so I had to change schools and move in with a family I barely knew. There was Nigel, his parents, his younger brother, David, and sister, Carol, and I missed my mother desperately.

But again, it was just what I had to do to make this work. If I go back in my mind and put myself in Mum's shoes, my whole body fills with anxiety.

Nigel was his mother's favourite. He was the superstar dancer and the golden child with a great job at the Bradford & Bingley building society and looked to have a bright future ahead. That bright future did indeed blossom as Nigel went on to become my financial advisor, a job he still does to this day. Lucky Nigel!

While I'll always be grateful to the Tiffanys for putting me up, I was undoubtedly the outsider and although my mother paid five pounds a week towards my room and board – everything she could manage – Mrs Tiffany, who absolutely ruled the roost, wouldn't allow me to use the little spin dryer Mum had given me because she said it cost too much electricity to run. Instead I'd have to hang my clothes out on the line.

She'd also count the potatoes she prepared in the pressure cooker to make sure I didn't pinch one, which I often did because as a growing girl I was permanently hungry! There was a lock on the landline so I couldn't use it, but I learned how to unpick it with a hair clip. I'd wait until everyone in the house was in bed and then creep down the stairs to call my mum (she had a telephone by then), holding down the dial as it wound back to reduce the noise, petrified someone would wake up and catch me.

My mother would pick up at her end and I'd whisper, 'Mum, I'm OK.'

Just hearing her voice was enough to carry me through the next few days.

Although there were periods where I was homesick and really quite down, it never occurred to me to quit. When you have a goal, something you believe in and feel is worth fighting for, you move heaven and earth to make it a reality.

'Every great dream begins with a dreamer. Always remember, you have within you the strength, the patience, and the passion to reach for the stars to change the world.'

HARRIET TUBMAN

Having been a bright, well-performing student at my school back home in Wallasey, when I moved to Shipley I fell behind, mainly because my focus was on dance and competing. Nigel and I would spend every weekend travelling up and down the country to take part in competitions and we were making good progress up the rankings. We would eventually perform a Viennese Waltz on the BBC's prestigious *Come Dancing* in 1977 when I was still only 16, so we were certainly good together.

I'd also started bunking off class, spending my days sleeping in the back of Nigel's yellow Mini while he went to work.

Unsurprisingly, my O-level results in 1976 were nothing to write home about and by then I couldn't wait to leave education behind, landing a job in a solicitor's office where my pay was 16 quid a week.

Now that I was earning my own money, it was down to me to pay Mrs Tiffany my room and board – if I ever got stuck, my mum would help with dresses or shoes, but I had to learn how to budget on that weekly wage.

I did this by writing lists. I still love a list. My mother had always written them for David and me ('go to the grocery store, peel the potatoes, put the food on by 5pm, tidy your room, bring the washing in') and I've carried that right through my life – although I know my obsession with them can drive other people mad!

Anyway, back then it was five pounds for two dance lessons and I'd have to pay Mrs Tiffany the fiver for my board. The six quid I had left would go to Nigel for petrol, perhaps some new rhinestones for my dresses, and I'd try if I could to put a little bit aside in the bank.

I should add here that by now, Nigel and I had fallen in love and planned to marry. We were just kids, of course, but he was solid, dependable and soft-natured and we were a team in every sense.

However, Mrs Tiffany was not happy when she discovered that our dance partnership had spilled over into romance. I felt I was never going to be good enough for her precious son and she blamed me entirely for the relationship, calling me every name under the sun and making me feel like I was in the wrong, ignoring the fact that it takes (ahem) two to tango! I've never quite understood how she worked that one out.

While the Tiffanys did eventually accept we were together as a couple, I was getting itchy feet in Yorkshire and knew that if we wanted to continue our trajectory then a move to London was going to be necessary.

We were already down there once a month to be taught by the famous Latin American coach Nina Hunt, and my friends Chris and Dawn Vickers had also recently made the move and were urging me to follow suit. I pretty much told Nigel I was moving to London with or without him.

My mother said I was bonkers. I was 16, I'd just got myself a good office job in Shipley and how on earth would I support myself in the capital city where I hardly knew a soul?

But somehow in my heart, I knew I would make it work. You know what happens when someone tells me I 'can't' …

I rented a room above The Nest restaurant in Norbury, south London, which was full of cockroaches and bugs that crawled up the walls. When you switched the lights out at night, you could hear them scurrying under the wallpaper and clattering across the floor.

God, it was grim. My front door was right by the bins. I can't remember how much rent I paid, but Dawn taught me how to live on a pound a day by going down to the market near closing time, just when the unsold meat and veg were going to get chucked. I'd get a job lot of veggies, stick it all in the pressure cooker and that's what would keep me going.

In a twist of fate, the flat was opposite Mick Stylianos's dance studio Top of the Stairs, which doubled up as a social venue and was one of the hottest night spots in London. I used to sit on my knees watching out the window as all the glamour pusses and the suited and booted queued to get in.

I couldn't afford to go myself – I was a nobody – but I used to drift away in a daydream, never knowing that years later I would not only teach in Mick's hallowed studio, but he'd prove to be my knight in shining armour when I got into a spot of financial difficulty.

It's unbelievable how life works out.

Nigel stayed up north until he managed to arrange a transfer with the building society to the Croydon branch in George Street and was able to join me. The job came with a flat, which meant no more cockroaches, and although it had no heating and was permanently freezing, it was ours.

What little savings I had were fast running out, though, and getting work myself was now paramount. The lady at the job centre informed me there was nothing available, but I had dance lessons to pay for and wasn't taking no for an answer.

'You've got to find me something,' I begged.

'The only job we've got is for a personal secretary and you certainly don't have the credentials.'

'Let me try for it anyway.'

It was nearly closing time and I think this woman just wanted to get rid of me so she could call it a day.

'Oh, go on then,' she said, rolling her eyes. 'You can go along and have the interview.'

And that's when I met Simon Byrne at paper merchants Parsons & Whittemore Lyddon Limited, to interview for a job which was way beyond my skill set even with my shorthand and touch-typing qualifications.

After looking at my sparse CV, he said, 'We'll be in touch.'

I knew what that meant. It was a polite rejection.

'No, please, you don't understand,' I replied. 'I can't leave your office without a job. Even if I'm cleaning toilets, I'll take it.'

He looked at me. My eyes were pleading.

There was a pause. Then a sigh.

'You know what?' he said, 'I'm going to give you a chance.' Bingo. He took me on as his PA.

There were three other secretaries in the office and they were all in their forties. I was a little dolly bird with the styled hair, tight-fitting collared T-shirts and miniskirts and I knew what those ladies thought of me.

And to be fair, I was a terrible secretary. I couldn't spell. I couldn't file. But it was another case of pushing with all my might to get to where I needed to be. My older and more experienced colleagues were laughing at me behind my back, but I just put a wall up because I absolutely had to keep that job to earn the money to support my dancing. That was the only thing that mattered to me.

Again, I get that stoicism and work ethic from my mother. No matter what – and my God, has she had a hell of a lot to withstand over the years – I have never known her not to work. She's 87 now so she could be forgiven for putting her feet up, but it's not in her nature.

Although she'd argue that taking care of me (as she does to this day) is a full-time job in itself!

'Your vision will become clear only when you can look into your own heart. Who looks outside, dreams; who looks inside, awakes.'

CARL JUNG

It was 1977 and I'd been in London for about six months when I was presented with the biggest dilemma of my life to date. But before I tell you about that, let me just step back and tell you a little about drive and ambition. It might help you understand why I made the decision I did.

Across all my decades in dance, an industry rife with wicked whispers and petty politics, I've had people questioning my abilities and doubting me as a person. And I know there are many who assume I've clambered over others to get to where I needed to go.

I'm fully aware that if I'm ever about to work with anyone new, somebody will pop up to warn them: 'Watch your back.'

Motsi Mabuse was told just that when she joined the *Strictly* judging panel in 2019 and I know who it was that tipped her off, too. It backfired on that particular person trying to stir the pot because Motsi, whom I've known for 25 years, is now one of my closest friends – I love the bones of that woman.

Someone else recently told me the same thing had happened to him – he was approached by someone I'd actually taught for a long time who advised him not to go into business with me, indicating that I wasn't to be trusted.

It's simply not true that I have ever used people or double-crossed them to climb the ladder. What I did was learn my trade. I studied hard. I educated myself about human nature first because I wanted to know what made people tick.

It was never just about the dancing for me – that was only part of it.

I hate to use the phrase stepping stones, because every person who has ever been in my life, bar one or two, I'm still in touch with and glad for their acquaintance.

Having said that, I definitely learned how to manipulate. Now, manipulation can come in many forms – it can certainly be a horrible way to treat people, but I wasn't that kind of operator. I turned certain situations to my advantage in order to move forward, but there was never any malice and I certainly haven't ever set out to hurt anyone.

If you want something badly enough, you can generally find a way to get where you need to go. That's what ambition means to me.

I've always tried to tread my own path and resist feeling envious of others who look like they have it better or easier or as if they've been given a leg up. Jealousy gets you nowhere – it can rob you of focus, stop you appreciating what you have, breed resentment and you can end up tearing yourself apart. And for what? Just because you perceive that someone has something you don't? Waste of energy.

I'll give you a good example. When we were kids, there was an annual competition at the iconic Hammersmith Palais where all the girls would parade in a circle and the judges would pick their Miss Ballroom Princess. I was always the one who went out in the first round while my friend Karen Johnstone (now Hilton) won it every year.

Karen and her sister Cheryl started dancing at the same time as me and those girls won everything. Karen was always gorgeous-looking with thick, dark hair, flawless skin and a tall, slender frame, and she came from a loving and comfortably-off family. Karen found herself a great dance partner in Marcus Hilton and the two of them became very successful – she remains one of the top females in our industry.

I used to look at her and think she had everything I wished I had, but I can honestly say that I *never* envied her. My mother had drummed it into me to banish what she called the 'Green Giant' otherwise I'd be setting myself up for a big disappointment.

Instead, what it did was build more resilience and drive in me. I didn't have what people like Karen had, so that meant I had to work that little bit harder all the time. Even now, I try to work just that bit harder today than I did yesterday.

And here's a thing. Karen has been in my life for 57 years now and we're virtually next-door neighbours in London. She came from a well-off family, I had a completely different start, but we've landed in the same place.

Funny, isn't it? It's not where you begin but how hard you're prepared to slog which will, ultimately, get you to your goal. In the end, it comes down to how much you want it, and what you're prepared to do to achieve it.

'There is no passion to be found playing small or in settling for a life that is less than the one you are capable of living.'

NELSON MANDELA

So back to 1977 and my dilemma. One day, my teacher, Nina Hunt, called me at work about a dancer named Sammy

Stopford, a Latin pro ranked seventh in the world who was looking for a new partner.

Knowing that I was interested in specialising in Latin, Nina pushed me to go for the try-out and told me I had until the end of the day to decide.

Of course, this put me in an agonising position with Nigel, who wasn't just my dance partner, but the man I thought I was going to marry. He was decent, kind and had been nothing but good to me. I couldn't bear the thought of hurting him.

On the other hand, I was 16, ambitious, and dancing was my whole life. And although Nigel and I had been fairly successful together, reaching the semi-finals in the closed British Ballroom championships and the second round in the Latin champion-ships, we weren't exactly setting the world alight. With hindsight, perhaps I should have had more patience but I was so desperate to be someone or something.

At the time I was ranked 96th in the world as an amateur and try-outs with dancers like Sammy were the sort of oppor-tunities that didn't come around very often. Even though merely attending would surely spell the end of my relationship with Nigel, I knew I'd be kicking myself if I didn't put myself in with a shout ...

I went along to the studio and within a few steps Sammy had made his decision.

'I'll take her.'

Just like that, he knew instantly. I think I did too because the chemistry on that dance floor was undeniable.

But I felt dreadful for Nigel, who was heartbroken when I told him. I did love him and insisted that although I had this new dance partner in Sammy, I didn't want us to break up as a couple.

That was my teenage naivete showing, because how could we possibly stay together after this?

Nigel was the right guy at the wrong time.

In dance, things move fast. Within 24 hours, I'd left the man I thought I loved, quit my job with Simon Byrne (something of a reprieve for him, given the fact I was such a bloody awful legal secretary who had made a total pig's ear of his filing system) and was moving to Manchester where Sammy was based to set up home with him and his male housemates.

Although all of this was difficult to get my head round and if I'd thought about it for too long, I might have had a meltdown, I tried not to look back and instead focused on getting to the top with Sammy.

We hit the ground running and got there quickly.

Sammy was a hard taskmaster whose standards were eye-wateringly high. But he was also a wonderful choreographer and taught me everything I needed to know about how the industry worked, including how to teach others. We'd practise for hours every morning and then teach in the afternoons to earn our living.

Somewhere along the line we became a couple off the dance floor too and, as was the norm in dance back then, we married in April 1980 when I was 19. Sammy and I travelled the world competing, coming third overall in the World Championships in Australia in 1980, second in the British Championships in 1982 and then being crowned British Open to the World champions in1983 at the age of 22.

A miracle.

This was what I'd worked my whole life for and was everything I'd ever wanted. I wonder what that seven-year-old girl at the Brownies who followed first the music and then her heart would have made of it all.

'Develop a passion for learning.
If you do, you will never cease to grow.'

ANTHONY J. D'ANGELO

My son Mark said something to me recently which really struck a chord.

'Have you ever sat down and asked Nan what she wanted to do in her life?'

Ouch. That hit me like a punch to the gut because it dawned on me that I never had. It hadn't ever even crossed my mind to ask her.

That night over dinner, I put the question to my mother and she told me that she'd wanted to be a tap dancer. She'd have liked, she said, to have been on the stage.

Whenever I pick her up for a little jig around the kitchen, she's very coordinated. My mother can't sing a note in tune, but she can move, she has a natural rhythm and I do wonder what might have been if she'd been given the opportunity to fulfil her dreams.

She'd actually been in tap classes when she was little, but her parents had taken her out to learn the piano instead, which she hated. A hobby is meant to bring joy, not feel like a chore or an obligation, isn't it? If you're forcing yourself to pursue something you don't enjoy, it's probably not worth it. Life's too short to spend time on activities that don't make you happy or challenge you in a way you can appreciate, or which don't bring you fulfilment.

Performing as a tap dancer is what my mother had wanted to do with all her heart. I felt sad for her (not that she'd ever want anyone's pity!) and bad that I'd never thought to ask her the question years before. We'll never know what it might have led to if she'd been given the chance to dance like she gave me.

They say if you find a job you love, you'll never work a day in your life. That's not strictly true because I have worked my socks off and shed blood, sweat and tears over my career, often at huge personal cost.

But going to work has never been a chore.

I wouldn't say I'm proud of myself; I'm not self-congratulatory, I don't sit there reminiscing about my achievements. And I'm not daft enough to get carried away thinking *Strictly* and the other TV opportunities will last forever.

That's why I'll never give up the day job – dance is my bread and butter and my first love. TV can be here today and gone tomorrow.

Take Arlene Phillips, for example, one of the most fabulous women I have ever come across. She's a world-renowned choreographer and was a judge on *Strictly Come Dancing* from the first series in 2004 until 2009 – you'll probably be familiar with the story of how she left the show, replaced by Alesha Dixon, the celebrity winner from two series previous in a move which sparked an ageism row that hit the headlines for months.

I watched it all play out from afar with a great deal of sorrow, but the way in which Arlene responded was remarkable. She rolled her sleeves up, carried on choreographing top West End shows, wrote a series of books and then, at the age of 78, became the oldest contestant ever to appear on *I'm a Celebrity … Get Me Out of Here!*

I went to watch her *Evening With …* theatre tour in 2021 where she spoke so candidly about everything she's achieved in her life and I found it inspirational. There is nothing that holds her back and she has done the lot – theatre, music videos, television, you name it – and is still in huge demand today. Gosh, if I can be half the woman she is at 82, I'll be more than happy.

Arlene's story is a good reminder of the unpredictability of TV, but also of the importance of keeping your options open.

Opportunities don't magically drop into your lap. If you sit around waiting for fate to do you a favour, you'll be waiting a long time. But if you put out that good energy, the universe has a way of responding, so that when one door slams shut, another one will open. You just have to be willing to push it.

Whether you're stepping onto the dance floor, into a new opportunity, or wrestling with a difficult decision, lean into your strengths and stay true to your values.

We are all capable of carving out our destiny.

Shirley's Shimmers

Follow what makes you curious,
not what you think you *should* be interested in.

✖

Identify what you're good at by keeping
going until you find it.

✖

If something makes your heart feel full,
it's worth fighting for.

✖

Celebrate all the small wins along the way.

✖

You don't need to be perfect at something;
if it brings you joy, it's serving a purpose.

✖

If you're willing to push through the challenges,
you might just have found your passion.

✖

Set small, achievable goals and be ready to
tweak them if life gets in the way.

✖

See setbacks as learning curves and
motivation to do better and to be better.

STEP TWO

Tell a Story

COMMUNICATION

'Straight spine,
walk in, say your bit,
don't take any shit.'

AUDREY

*A*t its core, dance is about communication. It's a universal language which cuts through barriers; it's the use of physical movement to set a scene and evoke emotion.

To tell a story.

The body and the energy become the voice and it's a powerful way to connect, because if the narrative is compelling and the dancer truly feels it, the audience will too. The importance of clear storytelling is something you'll often hear me and my fellow *Strictly* judges bang on about in our feedback to the celebrities – you can have all the technical ability in the world but you can't bring a piece of choreography to life unless you're able to express the inspiration behind it.

Being an effective communicator off the dance floor draws on much of the same awareness: it's body language, presence, tone and timing. How we show love, navigate conflict, form connections … it's all choreography.

I'm a straight shooter. I like to get things out in the open and so I will tell you how the land lies, no sugarcoating, no messing about, I'll say it how it is. I can't allow ill feeling to fester; if I did, I wouldn't be able to function. I hear of parents who say they don't talk to their kids and I could never do that with my son. I'd have a nervous breakdown.

If I've got an issue with anyone, I'll say whatever I need to, we clear the air and we move on.

Back when my second husband, Corky Ballas, and I were representing the United States in a competition in America, Sam Sodano, who is a ballroom legend and was on the judging panel that day, had marked us fourth in the Jive.

This was November and we were preparing to compete in Blackpool the following May, so we needed to work on whatever it was he'd marked us down on.

There was only one way to find out.

Sam saw me coming across the room and I later found out he'd whispered to the other judges, 'Watch out, she's on the warpath.'

I looked at him straight and said, 'I don't want you to mark me higher. I just want to know what you didn't like.'

He gave me his opinion, I took it away with me and Corky and I ended up winning the Jive at Blackpool. That's where clear communication can take you.

This hasn't always been the case, though, and it took me many years to find the confidence to speak up. When I was married to Sammy, I don't ever remember being part of any decision involving us as a couple or a dance partnership because he very much ran the show, and quite rightly so.

It was logical that he took the reins – he was much more experienced than me. I was just a kid when we teamed up, a teenager barely out of school, while he was seventh in the world, a master of his trade and entirely at home on the international stage.

I became used to other people telling me what to do, casting me in their mould and making it clear I wasn't entitled to an opinion, and of course I wasn't – I was just starting out on my journey. I hardly knew anything. Only when I look back *now* do I realise I felt institutionalised. It was a mental conditioning which felt quite suffocating, but, being so young, I never questioned it.

Sammy and I never had time to do anything outside of dancing and we only got married because our dance teacher told us we would sound great billed as 'Sammy and Shirley Stopford, the Non-stop Stopfords'.

I wasn't going off feelings because I don't think I had many of them back then.

Sammy and I have had our ups and downs over the years, but I will always be grateful for what he taught me and, despite everything, somehow we seem to gravitate to each other. Or maybe I gravitate towards him. If I was ill or needed him, I know in my heart that Sammy would be there for me in a New York minute.

But the years of being silenced took a long time to eradicate and I have to credit Corky for teaching me about mental strength. I thought I knew resilience until I met him – boy, did he make me realise I'd only scratched the surface.

You'll be hearing a lot more about Corky Ballas later, but some of his outspokenness and self-confidence rubbed off on me in the years we were together and, to put it bluntly, I don't take shit any more.

A case in point: shortly before my second series of *Strictly* in 2018, I was travelling back to the UK from LA and when the plane landed I noticed I had 15 missed calls from my fellow judge Craig Revel Horwood.

Odd. He obviously really needed to speak to me, so I knew something was cooking.

When I eventually found a quiet space to sit down and contact him back, Craig was not his usual larger-than-life self.

'Shirley,' he said sheepishly, 'I was doing a dinner-party speech last night and may have said a few things which were out of turn. It's not a big deal, but I thought you should know.'

It sounded fairly innocuous, although I didn't really know what to expect until the next day when his comments about my breasts were plastered all over the front pages of the tabloids.

Diaries were emptied and a 'clear the air' meeting was arranged for the following day, but although I was furious over what Craig had done, there was no point going in there all guns blazing. Anger and high emotion are counterproductive to good communication in my book because your message gets lost in the noise. My objective was to speak calmly but to make it clear how his comments had made me feel and why it should never happen again.

At that meeting, I locked eyes with Craig and said to him, 'I need a safe place to go to work, and I need people around me I can trust. I'll have your back if you've got mine, but I'm not here to be somebody's punchline, and I don't want to come into work worried about anything I do or say getting repeated. I don't need a man to make me feel horrible about myself; I'm perfectly capable of doing that on my own.'

I didn't need to labour the point any further.

Craig apologised profusely, owned what he'd done, sent me flowers and we moved on. We've had a brilliant relationship ever since and I respect him for taking accountability for what happened.

If you've got something important to discuss or there's a difficult conversation to be had, do it in person. The message is infinitely better when delivered that way because there's no mistaking tone – you can see the other person's body language and facial expression and read all those non-verbal communication cues which leave very little room for misinterpretation.

Why can't people talk to each other any more? Every discussion seems to be conducted over text, emails or – worst of all – voice notes. I don't like it. There's no substitute for face to face and being fully engaged when you're talking. If I ask someone how they are, it's not a mindless, kneejerk question. I listen to the answer. Why bother asking unless you really want to know? Give people a few minutes of your time, make eye contact and have a proper dialogue.

The way we broach uncomfortable conversations (which we all have to have at various points) is key. I'm not frightened to approach anyone if I think they might have been speaking out of turn, but I don't accuse, fly off the handle or raise my voice.

I've been pinned into a corner with a finger wagging in my face throughout my career and I've learned through a combination of that experience, a lot of reading and a ton of therapy that it serves no one.

Instead, I say, 'This is what I've heard. I won't believe anything until I hear it from you.'

If I need to get my porcupine bristles out, I will. But I don't bear grudges either and once I've said my bit, that's it done as far as I'm concerned.

There's a Buddhist saying which I think nicely sums it up: 'Holding on to anger is like grasping a hot coal with the intent of throwing it at someone else; you are the one who gets burned.'

It's up to the other person whether they choose to stay talking to me, but I will let go of my own emotion from there because life is hurtling along too fast to hang on to a grievance.

At this age, it's like a bullet train.

'Stand up for what is right, even if that means standing alone.'

SUZY KASSEM

There's a temptation, especially in anger, to jump in feet first and lash out. But allowing emotion to take over is no way to resolve conflict and rarely leads to a satisfactory outcome. Always pick your moment.

When I was younger, I'd get myself worked up like a coiled spring and then unleash without thinking. Now I take a step back, have a minute to reflect and only then do I deal with the situation in hand.

This was tested when I appeared on *Celebrity Bear Hunt* earlier this year. If you haven't seen the Netflix show hosted by Bear Grylls and Holly Willoughby, the premise of it was to take lots of people in the public eye and throw them into the Costa Rican jungle. The group was set a series of physical challenges and after each one, four of the losing celebs were selected to head to the dreaded Bear Pit where they had to evade capture by Bear, who was in hot pursuit. Of the people he managed to catch, one got sent home.

You never know how these things are going to be edited –
one misplaced word to which someone somewhere takes offence
and you can find yourself in the middle of a media storm with
your reputation, career and everything you've worked for hanging in the balance.

No wonder people are scared to express an opinion these
days – even Craig Revel Horwood has toned down his critiques
on *Strictly* recently.

But it's not fair when continuous bad behaviour that is
impacting on an entire group is allowed to go unchecked, and
there comes a point where you have to stand up for what's right.
I held my tongue until I could do so no longer.

Before we come to the moment that I decided enough was
enough, I'll give you a bit of behind-the-scenes background,
because I didn't get off to the most positive of starts on *Celebrity Bear
Hunt*. On the first day we were all on the bus waiting to be taken
to the camp which would be our home for the duration of our time
on the show. Everyone was there on schedule except one person.

We waited and waited. We hadn't been told the full cast of
names at that point, so none of us knew who it was that couldn't
get their lazy ass out of bed, but half an hour turned into an
hour which turned into two.

I wasn't the highest-ranked celebrity on that show – there were
other stars such as Boris Becker and Laurence Llewelyn-Bowen
who were bigger names than me, but this was getting ridiculous
and so I took it upon myself to raise it with the producer.

'The one thing in my life I can't replace is time,' I said. 'We
all have choices. And I don't choose to sit here in the heat waiting for whoever it is to turn up.'

Being late is the height of rudeness. It shows you have little to no respect for the people who you're forcing to hang about. I won't name and shame who it was with the dreadful timekeeping, but their car eventually pulled up more than two hours after we had been due to set off, so it wasn't the best of first impressions.

However, I'm all for giving people a chance and was very open to getting to know everyone there. I try to see the best in all humans and to search for the common ground even if it's not immediately obvious. And as a result, I had some wonderfully enriching conversations with my fellow campmates, people from different walks of life with fascinating stories and insight to share. I loved getting to know Boris Becker, Lottie Moss, Steph McGovern and Danny Cipriani over late-night deep and meaningfuls.

One of my campmates was Mel B from the Spice Girls. We sat talking on the bed one evening and had a reasonably pleasant chat where I asked her about her life and career. But I think she took a dislike to me because she believed I was being given an unfair advantage, having avoided being sent to the Bear Pit after a few days. She said it was because I was being protected and getting treated differently to the rest of them and she probably assumed that was because of my age. But none of that was down to me – Bear Grylls (and the producers) were the ones who decided which celebrities would go into the Pit each day.

I'm made of tough stuff and that sort of nonsense is water off a duck's back to me these days, but I watched her set about other people too. A classic tactic of hers was to say something horrible about someone and then follow the remark up with, 'Oh, but I'm only *joking* ...' as if that made it all OK.

It was all starting to make people feel very uncomfortable on and off camera and I knew there was going to come a point where I couldn't let it pass any longer. I've had plenty of practice in my life dealing with diva behaviour, so I knew to let it play out before choosing the right moment to pull her up. She might be called Scary Spice but she didn't scare me and if you watched the series, you'll have seen it was episode four when I confronted her.

Mel was having a conversation with the rapper Big Zuu when she turned to me and said, 'Yeah, we all have to go in the Pit *sometime*, Shirley.'

'Excuse me?' I replied.

She repeated the same dig back at me.

'You have to go into the Pit sometime, *Shirley*,' she said, putting the emphasis on my name to make it clear she was referring specifically to me.

I asked her what the matter was.

'I'm just saying …' she said.

'Mel, I'm not frightened of going into the Pit so I'm not sure what the issue is here,' I said.

'I'm just *talking* to you.'

'But you don't really "talk" do you, Mel? You're very direct and in people's faces.'

That prompted an outburst from her – Mel was clearly not used to being challenged – but I kept my cool.

'You don't have a great way of delivering a message,' I said.

'Neither do YOU!' she boomed back.

I was done.

Say your piece, keep it short and then walk away. You actually hear me mutter at the end of the exchange that I'm going to get my bug spray and go to bed. That's what I did, I had nothing more to say and I certainly wasn't going to fuel her fire and give her the satisfaction of being able to carry on kicking off.

She kept out of my way after that and we managed to remain civil but we're not going to be on each other's Christmas card lists.

I don't think Mel will ever change – that's just what she's like and I know she has been through some tremendously difficult times in her life which may well have shaped who she's become. Then again, haven't we all? It doesn't give you the right to be rude to other people.

I'm glad I said my bit and I think the atmosphere shifted for the better after our heated conversation, with Mel noticeably easing off the attitude.

An important lesson I learned later in life is never to get too far out of your lane, because you can only be responsible for yourself and sometimes it's not your job to speak up. But when I feel it's appropriate, I will always call out a bully when I see one.

'Conflict is inevitable, but combat is optional.'

MAX LUCADO

Sometimes you can let people dig their own grave. A dignified silence can often speak far louder than words and knowing when to deploy it is a powerful skill.

I've said many times that no one is bigger than *Strictly Come Dancing*, including myself. But unfortunately certain people can get entitled and start to think they're the big cheese. And, well, they tend not to last too long …

Brendan Cole was one of the show's original professionals, having been there since the first series in 2004, and was known as the bad boy of *Strictly* thanks to his regular run-ins with the judges, whom he was prone to challenging live on air if he disagreed with their critique.

I actually taught Brendan for quite a long time back in the day, but before my first show he'd appeared on the spin-off *It Takes Two* where he'd expressed some scepticism about my appointment. When host Zoe Ball asked him if all the pros were going to be 'desperate to impress' me, he pompously fired back that it was *me* who should be looking to impress *them* because they'd all been there much longer.

That set the tone and he paved the way to disaster from there. Not many people know that Brendan had also screen tested for Len Goodman's job on the *Strictly* judging panel at the same time as me, but he obviously hadn't got the gig and I wonder now if he was smarting from the fact I'd been chosen over him.

That would certainly explain a lot.

I know Anton Du Beke had advised him to go with the flow and accept the BBC's decision but for whatever reason he wouldn't. Or perhaps couldn't.

I felt that he was trying anything and everything to put me down, and it had all been bubbling away for quite a while before it finally blew up in week three as I was giving him and his celebrity partner Charlotte Hawkins their feedback.

I told them, quite correctly, that their Tango had rise and fall, which isn't supposed to be a feature of that dance. It was constructive criticism and I made the remark alongside some positive comments, but Brendan wasn't happy.

'I'm really sorry,' he said, passive aggressively, 'but there was no rise and fall in that whatsoever.'

'You should play it back, Brendan,' I advised, coolly.

'I will, my dear, I will.'

That crossed a line. The 'dear' was deliberate, it was patronising and rude and my fellow judge Bruno Tonioli stood up and warned him not to speak to me like that.

The people watching at home didn't like it either. Viewers knew that I was the newbie and their hearts and sympathy were with me. Brendan and Charlotte were in the bottom two the following week and were voted out unanimously by the judges.

I don't even know what possessed him to do that, unless he was so blinded by bitterness having thought he was going to get Len's job only for me to nick off with his big chance.

Whatever it was, I chose not to respond to the media requests for a comment and remained civil to Brendan when I next saw him. I kept my head held high.

And in the end that was to be Brendan's final year on the show. I watched him break the news of his departure on *Lorraine* and had a lot of empathy for him because he was understandably emotional.

Credit to Brendan, he went on to rebuild his career in TV and on the stage and I know he did *I'm a Celebrity … Get Me Out of Here!* and *Dancing on Ice* – two huge ITV shows.

I actually went to see his tour last year, which I enjoyed, and we exchanged pleasantries afterwards.

I mean it when I say I don't bear grudges.

> *'People will forget what you said, people will forget what you did, but people will never forget how you made them feel.'*
>
> MAYA ANGELOU

Not many people know the real me. The real Shirley. There are only a few who have been truly let into my life.

That doesn't mean I'm a closed book. Far from it. I thrive on human connection and I don't go anywhere without talking to people, whether it's the person on the door, the stage manager or the lady making the tea. I see others walk around all aloof as if they're the king or queen of England – you get a lot of superiority complexes in TV and in my world of dance.

But I am selective about who I show my vulnerabilities to and if I feel anyone is getting too close, I put barriers up. For *Strictly* I had to learn to take some of them down.

Those walls of self-preservation built up over a lifetime of hard knocks weren't right for a family entertainment show where you have to be open, relatable and accessible, not on guard and defensive.

So before that first series, producers paired me up with a marvellous TV coach called Francesca Kasteliz, who gave me a crash course in all things media and chipped away at my outer shell, helping me to loosen up and soften around the edges.

I knew I wanted to be feisty, fun and fair – the three Fs – and Francesca helped me develop that persona and work out ways of getting my message across in the 15 seconds I had to give feedback. I always judge without fear or favour.

I had often sat in the *Dancing with the Stars* studio over in America watching my son perform and I'd listened to judges Len, Bruno Tonioli and Carrie Ann Inaba's critiques, pondering how I might have delivered them differently. Sometimes I'd think, 'Do you realise that poor lad has just spent a 40-hour week working on this routine?' and all those experiences went into the melting pot which shaped me into the judge I am today.

Just like my private students, I always want the *Strictly* contestants to walk off that dance floor feeling as if there's hope. I can't guarantee anything about the future, I haven't got a crystal ball, but as long as there's hope you can move forward and progress.

Always at the forefront of my mind is how the people on the end of my comments feel. How is it going to affect them if I say X, Y or Z? *Strictly* isn't the World Championships; none of our celebrities are competing for a British or international title, for goodness sake. These guys are putting on their dancing shoes for three months if they're lucky, so my job is to give them some positivity and a few tools they can use to make it through another week.

I think very carefully about how I'm going to single out something they did well and something they can improve on along with a quick demonstration of how to do it. Nailing that is a skill I've had to learn and I'm still perfecting it.

Having been one of the *Dancing with the Stars* professionals since 2007, my son Mark appeared as a guest judge there in 2024 and he has a natural ability to deliver feedback in that succinct way. I was so impressed with him when I watched.

Of course, I've got the signature lines like 'It's never too early for a ten from Shirley', but I'm always trying to find original and creative ways to critique. I use the same technical feedback as I do for the top professionals in the world, although obviously I dilute it down and think of people like my mum sitting at home. Would she understand what I'm talking about? It has to be accessible to everyone.

For me, that celebrity is unique. When I'm deciding what I'm going to say, I start with the feet, I move up to the leg, I go to the hips and then on to the flexibility in the body. I go to the coordination and synchronisation of the arms, the postural line of the neck and the shoulders.

And then I look at how they've delivered their message and whereabouts in the series we are. If it's the first few weeks, I might focus on the feet and let the arms slide.

By the time it comes to the last three weeks, I'm not really talking about the technique any more because by then it's too late. Then it becomes about the show that they've put on, the performance as a whole and the chemistry they have with their partner.

As we see in every final, the ones who have made it that far always have a good standard of footwork, decent leg and body action and nice coordination in the arms. Plus personalities to die for.

I still value Francesca's input. I take on board everything she says and don't worry that her comments mean I'm not doing a good job. I'm always willing to listen to feedback and improve my game and she's particularly good at helping me switch hats because I wear so many. Every year I come to *Strictly* off the back of the International Championships at the Royal Albert Hall where I've been preparing professional dancers for this global competition – they need direction and tough love. Having been totally immersed in my professional world, I need to adopt a different approach for *Strictly*. She works with me to take the edge off and loosen up and she's so clever at what she does.

Last year it was suggested the judges increased their interaction with each other, so none of our mics were muted when we weren't talking, meaning we could interject. I enjoyed the freedom and the new dynamic it created, even though some people at home seemed to take it awfully personally, which was very amusing.

'How dare you interrupt Craig!' We got a few comments like that.

You're never going to please everyone all of the time, so it's best to stop trying.

'If we don't tell our own stories, we'll never take control of the narrative.'

JULIE CLARK

The very first press interview I did was with the *Sun* back in 2017, just as my world was about to be turned upside down with *Strictly*. The idea of the chat was to introduce me to the public ahead of the launch show and it was a positive piece, a good overall experience for my newspaper debut.

Afterwards, the journalist gave me some good advice which I've lived by ever since.

He said that if I wanted to enjoy a healthy relationship with the media – which of course I absolutely did – I had to learn to control the narrative.

'Are we going to catch you falling out of a nightclub, Shirley?' he asked.

'Certainly not,' I replied. 'I'll be the one holding the coats.'

He told me that as long as I was always honest, up front and made sure that I got in ahead of any story, then I wouldn't go far wrong.

For example, if I was planning on having a facelift, I should come out and say so – that way it's not a big shock and no one gives two hoots when it actually happens. The worst thing you can possibly do is lie or try to hide it because it's not a matter of 'if' it will come out, it's 'when'.

Which is precisely why when I had my 17-year-old breast implants taken out in 2019 due to health concerns around the history of cancer in my family, I was completely open about my plans with the media.

I did an organised sit-down chat with the *Sun* beforehand and then a week after the surgery I went on *Lorraine* to discuss the operation and my recovery. I did *Strictly* as usual in between all that, having refused to take the weekend off, but that's a story I'll tell you about later.

My honesty policy has served me pretty well over the years and I've always enjoyed a good relationship with the press who, on the whole, have been fair to me. I try to be as transparent as I can.

That doesn't mean I lay everything out there. If I'm asked something extremely personal or about, let's say, a *Strictly* 'controversy' I can't comment on, I choose diplomacy and swerve it because I would quite like to remain employed, thank you very much.

Neither do I feel obliged to answer intrusive questions from journalists. I did an article once, I won't say for which publication, and the opening line from the interviewer was, 'Can you tell us about your sex life?'

For a start, that wasn't even what the interview was supposed to be about, and secondly, I was sitting in hair and makeup when she asked.

I mean, at least let me get my glam on first!

I did get a little sharp with this lady and told her it was none of her business. She went away and wrote an article about me being difficult, ignoring the fact that she'd asked inappropriate questions I hadn't been prepared for. Why would anyone want to know about my life between the sheets anyway?

I have always tried to tell every part of my story so far as candidly as possible and I hope you feel that you know me well by now.

And if I ever do have that facelift, you'll be the first to know.

Shirley's Shimmers

Accept feedback in the spirit it's given rather than getting defensive. See it as an opportunity to be better.

✗

Remember that people appreciate and respond better to honesty and vulnerability rather than perfection.

✗

Resentment weighs you down,
so don't let it fester – speak up or let it go.

✗

Express concerns calmly and aim
to diffuse rather than fuel.

✗

There is power in silence.
Sometimes a pause for breath before you
respond can change the game for the better.

✗

If a conversation is worth having, face to face is always
the most effective for getting your message across.

✗

The truth isn't always pretty, but it's always real.

STEP THREE

Polish Your Stage Presence

CONFIDENCE

'Hang your problems at the door, darling, and pick them up on your way out.'

AUDREY

*A*s a performer, your command of the stage is critical. Stage presence is what captivates your audience and will have them eating out of the palm of your hand.

It's that star quality – the *je ne sais quoi* – that will set you apart. You have to own that space.

I'll let you in on a little secret. When the *Strictly* theme music strikes up and millions of people in living rooms across the country are waiting for the magic to start, my heart is pounding in my chest. Even now with eight series under my belt.

As my fellow judges and I are introduced one by one, strutting our stuff across the studio floor, I'm dolled up to the max – hair and makeup immaculate (thank you, Sven and Jane) and dressed in a fabulous frock (thank you, Alexandria).

Straight spine. Shoulders back. Smile, smile, smile.

I'm sure most of the people watching would assume here was a confident, self-assured woman entirely at ease in her own skin, but they'd be sorely mistaken.

That's something I'm still working on and most likely will be until I Samba off this mortal coil.

The thing is, I work in a job that requires a great deal of 'confidence' to get where you need to go, so I'm a bit like a trained monkey in that respect.

Put me out there and I know how to deliver.

Give me a stage and I'll perform.

Show me to a red carpet and I'll work that camera as if my life depended on it.

But none of that is down to self-confidence. That's about knowing how to put on a show – it's me slipping into a role, one I play extremely well.

I have an invisible red button which sits on my left shoulder. Just before the *Strictly* studio lights go up or I step out of the car at an event, I push that button and I'm on.

Lights, camera, action.

Just the other day, I was leaving a hotel where there were paparazzi outside. I was feeling particularly stressed about a personal matter and my PA Harry just looked at me because he knew.

'You OK?' he asked. 'Press the red button.'

'Let's do it,' I replied.

I lifted my head, took a deep breath, allowed a dazzling smile to spread across my lips and Shirley Ballas walked out the doors.

It was the same when I was competing – as soon as I took to the dance floor, it was as if I became a separate person. I guess that red button did a pretty good job as it helped me become British champion at 22, British Open to the World champion three times with two different partners, three times European, International and United Kingdom champion and ten times Open to the World United States champion.

But it also means that a lot of the time I'm hiding behind a mask and outside of the spotlight it's a different story. The confidence I wear is only borrowed and believe me, when I'm on my own it can all crumble to dust.

My struggles with self-esteem began in my early teens when I developed acne, an issue I was constantly and painfully aware of.

There was an older girl who danced at the same studio and she had very badly pock-marked skin – she suffered a lot and was called multiple names – and one mother kindly informed me I was going to end up just like her.

'See that girl over there – that'll be you in a few years' time, Shirley Rich.'

That was terrifying to me, not just because I was self-conscious enough and didn't want to contemplate this being a lifelong affliction, but also for my future in an industry which was all about comparison with an intense focus on appearance. These very deliberate little digs about the way I looked chiselled away at my self-worth and would become deep-set insecurities I'm still grappling with today in my sixties.

I wasn't ever one of the 'pretty' girls. If I went to the local youth club, it wasn't me the boys would flock round. It was the other girls with their lovely hair and blue eyes and the latest fashions.

I'd always be the one hanging back, looking in.

I suppose I was what you might call a late bloomer, but I never considered myself to be that attractive. As well as the spots on my face, I'd get nasty comments about the mole on my chin, my thin hair and crooked teeth. Nothing ever seemed to be right.

I spent years thinking I needed to be fixed … I can see now I was never broken to begin with, but embedded feelings of inadequacy are difficult to erase completely.

Like I say, I'm working on it.

'Self-confidence can be learned, practised, and mastered, just like any other skill. Once you master it, everything in your life will change for the better.'

BARRIE DAVENPORT

If you're not feeling it, fake it. That's a little trick which works (just about) every time. It's what got me through the initial *Strictly* hysteria when I made my debut on the show in September 2017, Samba-ing my way onto the famous dance floor, knees shaking, the sweat seeping out of me and so nervous that I thought I might keel over.

Live telly was something way out of my comfort zone – I was wracked with self-doubt and I didn't know whether the public were going to take to a middle-aged, inexperienced, television newbie.

I thought trying to fill the departing head judge Len Goodman's shoes would be very difficult indeed, if not impossible. Lovely Len had such a distinctive turn of phrase, he was so clever with the way he expressed himself and he'd been part of the *Strictly* fabric since the show began back in 2004.

I had no idea how I was going to avoid getting tongue-tied knowing that ten million pairs of eyeballs were waiting for me to trip up.

On top of all this, I'd fallen into the foolish trap of comparing myself to the ever-so beautiful Darcey Bussell who would be sitting alongside me on the panel. She'd been with the show since 2012 and as a former prima ballerina at the Royal Ballet, she was the epitome of elegance.

Graceful, beautiful, well-spoken and stunningly gorgeous, she had such poise and just being in her presence, you felt an aura.

I tore myself apart thinking about how I was going to be perceived sitting next to her. I saw myself as the Ugly Sister and Darcey as the classy Cinderella and every insecurity I'd been haunted by my whole life came rushing to the fore.

In the weeks before my first show I practically starved myself in a bid to look somewhere near to half-decent, dropping a lot of weight very quickly. If you go back and look at pictures from that time, you'll see I'm half the size I am now.

I might have got into the slinky, figure-hugging red dress I wore for the launch where I was introduced to the audience for the first time, but at what price? Sure, I was thinner than I had been in years, but I was also deeply unhappy and bloody hungry.

It was miserable, I couldn't have maintained it and if I could travel back in time I'd give my head a thoroughly good wobble.

The torture we put ourselves through …

Well. Darcey was a total dream to work with. She taught me the ropes, telling me having another woman on the panel to make it 50–50 for the first time was 'strength in numbers'. She was so kind, a genuinely lovely human being and a great judge across the years she spent on the show.

And while I'd thought she was perfection on pins with a charmed existence, I later learned that Darcey had been going through quite a hard time herself at the time she'd started on the show and I'm sure she's fought plenty of personal battles to get to where she is. Meeting and getting to know her was a good lesson in why we should never make assumptions about anyone because we don't know what is going on behind the scenes.

Everyone has their crosses to bear.

What a pointless waste of time it is comparing ourselves to other people. We are who we are and we should celebrate all the things that make us different.

And I'm not sitting here claiming to have all this figured out. Not by a long shot! I'm still susceptible to it – comparison is a natural human tendency and one that's hardwired into our psyches.

Case in point: someone in my circle had been watching *Strictly* recently and told me that they felt my commentary was 'a little bit flat' compared to my fellow judge Motsi Mabuse, who was much more excitable and expressive with her body language.

This person didn't mean any harm, but their remarks got me thinking (overthinking would be a more accurate way of putting it) and so the next week I switched it around and tried to oomph up my critiques.

Unlike Motsi, I took it too far. I was full of this performative exuberance, flinging my arms about and standing up out of my seat ... but when I played it back, I was mortified. I thought I looked flipping ridiculous. In fact, so ridiculous that people on Twitter were comparing me to a crane because I was on my feet and looking over the desk that much!

Motsi and I both bring something unique to the panel and it's our differences that make the whole team work so brilliantly.

As head judge, I see myself as a voice of authority, I'm there to provide an appraisal of the movement from top to bottom, drawing on my expertise from nearly 60 years in dance and to offer encouragement for the week ahead.

So you see, *Strictly* is not just a job for me, it's been a place of learning and I'm always looking for new ways to express myself, things I can do to come across more clearly and deliver the feedback constructively while keeping it entertaining.

But I will remain true to myself and who I am while doing so.

Which brings me back to something I remember thinking right at the beginning of my *Strictly* journey when I was fretting about the task of replacing Len Goodman.

Of course I couldn't fill Len's shoes. I could only put my own fluffy slippers next to them.

'Your body is the piece of the universe you've been given, the place where love and joy and grief happen, so honour it.'

GENEEN ROTH

There's no getting away from it, the pressure women everywhere face to look a certain way is immense. You can multiply that by about a zillion in the dance industry.

I've seen extremely talented people quit after being told they needed a facelift or because they were deemed overweight. There's an obsession with body fat percentage in dance – woe betide if I ever had any so-called 'jiggly bits' – so it's hardly surprising that this fixation has created a culture where eating disorders are rife.

Dancers are measured not just by their technique but by their physique, and their bodies are constantly scrutinised to the point where they can push themselves to extremes, restricting food intake and overtraining to shrink their weight and body fat to the bare minimum. I've seen it happen.

The pressure starts early, with young girls absorbing messages from right across the board that 'thinner is better' and success is only possible if you're super slim. They tell me they feel happiest when they're emaciated, which is a shocking state of affairs.

People say it shouldn't be about that but unfortunately my industry is still stuck in the Dark Ages and weight still plays a vital role in a dancer's success.

I've not been immune to any of that and body image is something I've battled for as long as I can remember. I'm not naturally thin – I have curves and gain weight easily – so I have to watch what I eat in order to keep unwanted pounds at bay.

When I was married to my first husband, it was made abundantly clear that to win at a professional level, I had to be a certain weight. He was a tough cookie and I don't think I ever felt quite good enough as either his dance partner or his wife. I found out years later that he did indeed have doubts about whether I was 'good enough' for him, professionally at least, so my instincts were correct. They usually are.

It was the same story when I danced professionally with my second husband; we were both made aware of our physiques and would put ourselves on extreme diets, like the time when we'd only consume grapefruit juice and I'd hope to get the bulk of the pulp so I could feel at least a little bit full.

Both of my ex-husbands had tiny waists and they weren't much taller than me and when people tell you that you've got a bigger bum than your male partner, those comments are taken to heart.

I've gone to great lengths in pursuit of the perfect body. I had the fat drained out of my arms and legs, a boob job and my teeth straightened, although none of it made me more confident.

Even now I don't walk past mirrors with no clothes on. What I can't see won't get to me.

I've not suffered an eating disorder, but I have been on every faddy diet under the sun and even once gave slimming pills a go because I was told they would help me get rid of bloating from water retention.

What I soon realised, though, is that the side effects with those things are pretty grim – increased heart rate, digestive issues and insomnia to name a few – and I didn't like what they did to my energy. They made me permanently jittery and unable to sit still or stay calm.

And now, of course, we've got these weight-loss injections that so many people are taking for a quick fix. It's such a worrying trend and over the last couple of years we've seen celebrities who were already very svelte, shrinking at breakneck speed. You might say it's the new drug of choice in the world of showbiz.

I was offered Ozempic and I have to confess that I did consider accepting it – I always feel like I have a stubborn four or five pounds to lose and those decades of pressure for perfection die hard.

The temptation was there, but in the end, I declined the offer mainly because I don't feel there's been enough research on what effect it might have on your organs. And the older I get, the more protective I am about what goes into my body.

I don't take chances with it.

I can understand why people go down the Ozempic route – like most things these days, everyone is looking for a shortcut solution, but weight loss doesn't have to be complicated. The simple truth is that if it goes in, it goes on and I always tell myself if I need to lose a few pounds, 'Shirley, dear, cut down on your portions and move that 65-year-old body.'

That doesn't mean surviving on kale, running a marathon and doing a few rounds of the Quickstep before breakfast. It's about making better food choices and staying consistent. Nothing is a substitute for facing what the real issue is and tackling it in a healthy way.

Having said that, it's definitely harder work keeping the weight off now compared to when I was a young teeny bopper. I remember my doctor saying to me at my annual check-up when I turned 50, 'Well, everything with a salad from here on in, Shirley …'

He said it with a twinkle in his eye and a smile, but when you're already predisposed to body-image issues, words like that hit hard.

I tend to yo-yo so I have to be very disciplined to ensure I don't allow myself to be a size 12. That's my red line. I make sure to stay a 10, although my preferred size is an 8 and if I feel like my clothes are getting a bit too tight for comfort, I know what I need to do.

That's when my mum will tell me, 'You've got five potatoes stuck in your knickers.' She's been telling me that for years so I'm almost immune to it when it comes from her.

I tend not to eat after 6pm and I've cut out most processed food. I try to eat chicken and four ounces of vegetables and sometimes I do intermittent fasting. If I want a 'treat', it's a conscious decision and only every so often. If I find myself reaching for that bar of chocolate, I stop and think twice.

But there's a difference between now and before. Years ago, I had breast surgery because I thought it would make me more desirable, always trying to mould myself into someone else's idea of perfection. Sod that. Now, I do everything for myself – nobody else – and that change is crucial.

I won't ever change myself again for validation in society, for male approval or because the world tells me I'd be more worthy if I took up less space.

If you're reading this now and feeling some of the pressures I've described, I hope you can take heart from the knowledge that you're not alone and start to feel better about yourself.

Our bodies fight for us every single day and they deserve kindness and compassion, not criticism and loathing.

'Never bend your head. Always hold it high. Look the world straight in the eye.'

HELEN KELLER

After my *Strictly* debut, one of the first people who came up to me was the TV presenter Eamonn Holmes. His then-wife Ruth Langsford was a celebrity contestant on that series and Eamonn approached me backstage, although I wasn't absolutely sure of who he was at the time.

He said, 'A lot of things are going to happen in this industry of TV, Shirley, but I want you to know that I thoroughly enjoyed listening to you tonight and it's great that you're part of the show.'

I looked him up online later and saw he was a superstar and I thought, 'Well if *he* thinks I'm quite good, maybe I should start believing in myself a bit more.'

Eamonn won't have realised how important his kind words were to me, but he gave me the confidence I needed to carry me through to the next week.

That's why I always take the time to pay someone a compliment or offer a bit of encouragement to anyone who might need it – it's a few seconds out of my day but I know how a small gesture like that can make a big impact.

People are often carrying burdens we know nothing about. When we lift each other up, we can start a ripple effect and help create a world where everybody feels valued.

We know that the mind and body are connected, so if you walk the walk, talk the talk, and act as if you have confidence, your brain will begin to believe it.

When you enter a room, lower your shoulders and put your game face on, and just by that self-assured posture, you can command attention. Even in situations I'm unsure about, I can always act like I'm in control and it all stems from my frame and deportment.

I might be absolutely terrified, but no one in that room would ever know.

The second you flinch or show signs of retreating back into your shell, people will read that you're nervous and the jig is up.

I think of it as a bit like how a lion or tiger might command space in the jungle.

No matter how I feel, I get up in the morning and put myself out there. I put on my big girl's pants, metaphorically and literally – there's something about big knickers which make me feel better, stronger. High-waisted, like a girdle, with nothing exposed and always from Marks & Spencer.

I put them on and I'm a superhero.

Then it's a little bit of makeup – a sweep of mascara and a slick of lipstick can work wonders on both the outside and in – and I don't go anywhere without my hair done. I'll wash and curl it even if I'm just getting straight into the car, because having it styled instantly lifts my spirits and makes me walk that little bit taller.

Trade secret for you: I also do it because there's often a photographer lurking somewhere waiting to capture me looking dishevelled and I refuse to let those pesky snappers get the shot!

When it comes to clothes, I have to feel comfortable and that, for me, is black leggings, a black blouse and black dance shoes for teaching and a suit or a dress if out to dinner. I always want to look respectable and that I've made an effort. Having said that, I like nothing more than slobbing about in a pair of sweatpants when I'm off duty.

'You should always look the best you can with the money you've got,' says my mother. It's a rule she's a stickler for and even now in her late eighties, whenever she goes out, she has a smart coat with a brooch – always a brooch – silk scarf, hair and makeup immaculate and nails painted to perfection. That's who she is.

'Make sure you leave the house wearing clean knickers and a nice bra just in case you're in an accident,' is another one of her gems. Even though it makes me laugh, it's advice I've always followed.

> 'No one can make you feel inferior without your consent.'
>
> ELEANOR ROOSEVELT

Right from my school days and then throughout my career in dance, bullies have been a persistent presence.

I was bullied in the playground for coming from a one-parent family and for being from the Leasowe estate. The kids would laugh at me for being a dancer and when I broke my foot doing the high jump in PE, they delighted in this, telling me I'd never dance again.

There wasn't one thing in particular which damaged my confidence and made me doubt myself, it was more like a constant swirl of derogatory comments from the other students and a lot of snobbery and judgement which I internalised and normalised.

So by the time I started to dance competitively, I was already used to being picked on and had built up a tolerance for that sort of behaviour. It escalated the older I got, but so did the increase in tolerance and I allowed it to happen because it had been part of my life all along.

I accepted it as routine.

It's no surprise that the mental health of so many dancers is hanging in the balance.

I see the manipulation. I see the bullying. The trouble is that the perpetrators are so used to doing it that it's become second nature and they're unable to step back and see themselves as the problem. The bullying men influence their wives and then the wives become an even bigger menace. We'll return to this later on because it's something that has long angered me and I'm finally ready to talk about it.

In the eyes of many, I'm a strong character and I know it's down to the resilience that comes from growing up on a housing estate. I'm quite able to take the brickbats, but dance industry misogynists have pushed me to breaking point. They tried to ruin me and, I have to admit, they very nearly succeeded.

After my second marriage ended, I set out on my own, starting from the bottom of the ladder to build a successful teaching business over the next several years. But there were plenty of people who couldn't stand to see a woman doing well. They felt I needed my wings clipped and were determined to bring me down by intimidating my students into leaving me.

The lowest point came around 2016 with Maurizio Vescovo, whom I'd been teaching for a long time. He was flying with me, really going places, but because certain people, these shadowy figures high up in the dance world, had decreed that I was getting too big for my boots, they decided to sabotage me.

The exact words they said to Maurizio were, 'There's nine of us, and one of her. If you stay with her, we'll make sure you'll never become world champion.'

Maurizio felt he had no choice but to leave. I remember I was in my apartment in California when he called me to say they'd got to him and scared him off.

I don't harbour any ill-feeling towards Maurizio – he was young and overawed – but guess what? He never went on to become a world champion. I'd helped him through the ranks from 48th to second in the world and that's where he retired.

I think losing him was when I realised some people are prepared to go way beyond the norms of humanity to put others down.

It was all so deliberate, these attempts to freeze me out.

Imagine being in a studio with a load of other teachers and having to watch the kids you taught dance to now being taught by someone else because they've been instructed not to speak to or train with you unless they want to risk their future in the industry.

Even an ex-boyfriend whom I'd been with for six years, couldn't bring himself to say hello to me when he came into the studio. His parents had raised him beautifully and he was always such a polite young man and so for him to be so ill-mannered beggared belief. My former students weren't allowed to talk to me, train with me, or be any part of my life, because they were terrified into submission.

In among all that, there were some people who had my back. John Kimmins, who is the former president of Arthur Murray International, which has dance studios all over the world, said to me, 'As long as I'm alive, you'll have a job with me, Shirley.'

He's a good man and has always been there for me throughout my dance career and beyond.

Many others knew what was going on but said nothing, perhaps assuming I was tenacious enough to come through it all. And in the end, I was – I always am – but it wasn't easy and I was incredibly vulnerable during this brutal period, which spanned several years.

I still find myself having to deal with shoddy male behaviour, whether it's invading my personal space, constant innuendos or the game-playing which means I've got to have eyes in the back of my head.

I did say one day the ship would sink and all the rats would fall off and that's exactly what happened, because since I've been on *Strictly* the very same people who tried to bury me are now charm incarnate.

I should probably thank them, because they forced me to be braver and better. And unapologetically me.

'You have to believe in yourself when no one else does – that makes you a winner right there.'

VENUS WILLIAMS

In my family, no one is allowed to play the victim. If it's ever sensed for one minute that I'm going that way, I'm stopped in my tracks. I will never succumb to self-pity because I know it will get me nowhere. I would only drown in my own sorrow.

I only wish I could go back and tell the younger Shirley that she was going to be OK. I wish I'd been able to believe in myself more, found my voice sooner and had the guts to fight back.

I should never have tolerated any of the bullying.

Apparently when I was little, I was quite outspoken and didn't like criticism. When the teacher put that in my report, my mother wrote a letter back saying it would be good if the woman could spell 'criticism' before she criticised.

But as I got older, I avoided conflict and lacked the courage to stand up and say how I felt. This is still work in progress for me and I can easily throw myself off course by overthinking, but I have tools in place now to help me through.

I have regular therapy, I practise yoga and meditation and I'm working on the way I talk to myself to make sure it's always positive.

Surrounding myself with good, kind, wise, like-minded people whom I can learn from is key. I choose my circle wisely these days.

I know people talk about me behind my back but nowadays I'm inclined just to let them get on with it. My mother told me recently that one of the greatest lessons she learned while working on the conveyor belts at the Cadbury's factory, was that the bravest person on the production line was the first one who dared to go to the toilet. That was because the others would immediately gossip about them when they'd gone.

That made me chuckle.

So, I no longer seek the validation of others. True stage presence isn't about being the loudest or most charismatic person in the room; it's about keeping your head held high and blocking out the noise.

It's pushing that red button and going on with the show.

Shirley's Shimmers

Practice makes perfect. When you act as if you belong in a space, eventually you'll feel like you do.

✗

Dress the part and carry yourself with self-assurance.

✗

Watch how you talk to yourself – switch the script and speak with the same kindness as you would a friend.

✗

Work on your body language: stand tall, shoulders back, make eye contact and move with purpose.

✗

Stop seeking validation.
Not everyone will like you, and that's OK!

✗

Forget other people's expectations.
You don't need approval from anyone else.

✗

Look after yourself, physically and mentally. Prioritise self-care – backing yourself is the best investment you can make.

✗

Learn to trust yourself, your judgement and your abilities – you are more capable than you think.

✗

Don't be a carbon copy of anybody else.

✗

Know you are enough. You've always been enough.

Be Confident Out of Hold

'It's all sent to try us.'

AUDREY

*B*eing able to dance out of hold without relying on a partner to lead is something many of our *Strictly* celebrities struggle with. It's completely understandable. When you're in the arms of a professional, you're held, you have structure and they will cover a multitude of sins for you. Going it alone means that the safety net is whipped away; it's exposing and raw and there's nowhere to hide.

Having confidence out of hold means nailing the posture and the balance enough to move independently without the physical contact of a partner ... I'm not sure I've quite conquered that away from the dance floor.

I've always had a terrible fear of being alone. I don't know where it started but it possibly stems from childhood anxieties.

'Once I leave you,' my mum would say to me and David as she headed out to work, 'put the bolt on and don't answer the door to anyone.'

All that is deeply ingrained and I'm sure it's at least partly why I am the way I am.

Perhaps it's also the feelings of abandonment which linger from my dad's absence as a parent. The broken promises, the rejection, the continued let-downs.

I don't care too much for my own company because it means I have to be alone with my thoughts. When I'm by myself, I start to overthink and small issues I'd normally be able to ignore grow into large, overwhelming ones.

Every 'what if' I've tried so hard to bury resurfaces and my mind takes me to my brother taking his own life and all the things I could and should have done differently. If I'd had a better understanding of mental health, he might still be here; if only I hadn't invited my mother down to London, leaving David up north on his own, perhaps all our lives would look very different today.

I ask myself the same questions over and over and my thoughts start to spiral, which is one of the reasons I work so hard and make sure my diary is always full. When my brain is occupied and I'm on the go, I can keep unhealthy ideas and intrusive thoughts in check. There's no space for them when I'm busy.

When I stop and I'm on my own – whoosh – that's when I torment myself. So, I tend to keep going, starting my day early and ploughing on until late at night. I know this probably isn't the healthiest solution and it's something I've been working on in therapy. But hey, there's a lifetime of trauma to unpick here.

I don't know if I'm co-dependent, but sharing my house with my mother is another self-preservation tactic, especially now I'm single again. I wish I could be one of those people who thrives in solitude and finds living alone empowering, but I never have been and never will be that person.

When my son and his best friend Derek Hough, a brilliant young dancer from Utah who had come to live and train with us in London, left for America in 2007 to join *Dancing with the Stars*, it was the first time I'd lived completely alone. My mum was living back in Wallasey, my second marriage was over and I was left rattling around in my house not knowing what to do with myself.

I detested that feeling, I hated the silence and being in the grip of this bleak loneliness. I hadn't lived in that house for very long so it didn't feel like home anyway, even less so without my family.

Leaving the UK had been a huge decision for Mark because it meant turning his back on competitive dance and pressing pause on a burgeoning West End career. He was only 21. But it was an amazing opportunity for him and impossible to turn down.

I didn't doubt for a second that he would make a good go of it.

Not only did Mark go on to be one of the most successful professionals ever on *Dancing with the Stars*, winning the series three times over his 20 seasons on the show, but he also became a leading light on Broadway and in 2016 was the final actor to play Frankie Valli in the long-running hit musical *Jersey Boys*.

I was, and still am, so proud of my son.

But although I was overjoyed that Mark was following his dreams, being alone in London was intolerable for me.

The empty nest syndrome raised merry hell with my emotions.

It took me about six months to realise I didn't want to live like this. I couldn't bear it, so I packed a bag and headed off to the United States. I rented an apartment in the heart of LA opposite the Grove shopping mall, people soon heard I was in town and my teaching business started to pick up.

My good friend Alan Grundy moved in with me (who I've known since he was a juvenile, junior and youth dancer, as well as during his amateur career where he ended up as British Open to the World champion. He was also crowned Hairdresser of the Year and it was he who named me the Queen of Latin). Life was changing. I was now in LA, living with my best friend in a lovely apartment and enjoying weekly visits to the *Dancing with the Stars* studio.

I know I'm a walking, talking contradiction because on the one hand I'm fiercely independent, completely self-sufficient and like to stand on my own two feet.

On the other, I need to be needed and always want someone with me.

I was engaged at 16, married to someone else at 19, divorced at 24, married again at 25 and had a baby at 26, so there was never time for me to discover who I was or establish an identity for myself without a partner. I didn't have a spell 'out of hold' until I was in my mid-forties and my second marriage had reached the point of no return.

I think so many people stay in terrible relationships and put up with appalling behaviour because the fear of being alone is greater than the pain of the toxicity in the marriage. It's easier to cling on to something broken yet familiar than face the alternative of nothing at all.

I get that.

I live with the constant worry that I'm going to be left alone one day, with no one to love me and no one to care about me.

'I'd rather love a million times and have my heart broken every time than hold a permanently empty heart forever.'

H.C. PAYE

I'm the first to admit that my love life is a disaster zone. I've lurched from one bad choice to another, been to hell and back and nursed a shattered heart more times than there are spins in a Viennese Waltz.

Sometimes I've wondered if it's me. Maybe I'm the sort of person who enjoys the excitement of a relationship at the beginning and then taps out when it wears thin.

I did Jamie Laing's podcast *Great Company* in 2024 and he asked me an intriguing question on this subject which started my mind whirring. He speculated on whether an absent father whose main contribution to my life was to let me down had impacted on my relationships with men.

Gosh. I'd never considered that before and it's something I have kept returning to ever since my conversation on that pod because it feels like the start of a bit of clarity. A penny-drop moment.

Now, I'm not blaming my messy, complicated personal life on my father, but I certainly never had any sort of paternal role model to go off.

If I was to compare myself to a particular friend of mine, the contrast is as clear-cut as you like. Her parents were inseparable and her dad was there to support her, to defend her and to show her how she should be treated by a man. He was a real snuggle bunny who always spoke to his children with respect – I never heard him raise his voice.

This friend has been married to her husband for over 40 years – she knew exactly what she should expect from a relationship and what she deserved because her father had set the example and she grew up seeing what a healthy, loving relationship looked like.

Go figure.

My mum is my rock and she gave me the ability to manoeuvre in different directions. But as mighty as she is, she could never be a substitute for a father and I often wonder what I may have missed out on. If anything at all. It's interesting that although I've learned something from every relationship, I have continued to make mistakes or ignore the warning signs until I'm in too deep, which I guess is why I'm on my own again at the age of 65.

Nigel was a good guy, but I broke his heart to dance with Sammy and headed north to begin the partnership that would take us to professional glory. I was only 17 and didn't know Sammy at all, but we had to share this room and while there was physical attraction, I don't believe there was any love. I don't think I had any idea what love even was back then.

In my head I knew he was a good partner for me as far as our dancing career was concerned and I saw very quickly that we were going places, but it was all very businesslike. I think I had one holiday with Sammy in all the years I was with him, we never went on dates and I didn't have an 18th or even a

21st birthday celebration because we were on a permanent hamster wheel where nothing mattered outside of dance and the next competition.

By my early twenties, all my youth had been spent working and my heart was yearning for something else, something more. Maybe if I'd communicated better to Sammy about how I was feeling we could have worked it out, but I didn't have a clue how to do that. I was just a young girl. I believe now, in my heart, that Sammy did love me, he just couldn't show it. I wanted fun, spontaneity and excitement in my life and that's what I found in Corky Ballas.

He crashed into my life like a human wrecking ball. It was February 1983 and I was in Canada with Sammy to compete in La Classique du Québec, a huge contest featuring dancers from all over the world.

After Sammy and I had taken part in and won our competition, we were introduced to Corky, an amateur dancer, and his professional partner Patrea – they'd won their pro-am event the previous day. Corky had been impressed with our performance and wanted to invite us to his hometown of Houston the following month to dance at the Texas Challenge.

We'd be well paid – Corky came from unfathomable wealth thanks to his entrepreneur father George, who had built a multi-million-dollar empire after inventing the Weed Eater device for trimming weeds around trees. The Ballases had also owned Dance City USA, the biggest dance studio in the world at the time – 43,000 square feet of dance floor. It was where Patrick Swayze had started out, no less. When George sold the place in 1970, he'd made millions.

Corky's invitation to Houston sounded like an extremely lucrative prospect for me and Sammy (he'd promised to pay us to teach eight lessons a day whether we worked or not) and we were both cock-a-hoop with excitement as we flew out to the States a few weeks later. In fact, it turned out to be a life-changing trip but not quite in the way any of us expected.

We were being put up in the Westchase Hilton, a hotel owned by the Ballases, which is where Sammy preferred to stay in watching movies when we weren't teaching or dancing. He wasn't interested in nights on the town.

I, on the other hand, was dazzled by the bright lights and the glamorous lifestyle the Ballas family led and Corky knew how to show a girl a good time. I loved his humour and the fact he was a free bird, a party boy. He was 21, the same age as me, and by the end of the week our flirting had become a passionate affair.

When Sammy and I returned to Manchester, we had to concentrate on and prepare for the British Open to the World championships in May, but all I could think about was Corky Ballas. We kept in touch with clandestine trans-Atlantic phone calls, he'd send me bouquets of flowers and on the eve of the championships, he told me he loved me for the first time.

I've no idea how I managed to focus on the competition to win all five dances and be crowned champions – a title Sammy and I had been working towards for five relentless years.

In the months that followed, Corky and I started meeting up whenever we could – he would sometimes jump on a plane from Texas just to spend a few stolen hours with me. The thrill of the chase was thrilling indeed, but this double life wasn't sustainable and eventually I had to confess to Sammy that I was in love with Corky.

He was understandably furious and stopped speaking to me, although only off the dance floor. On it, we continued to perform and no one would have ever known. Dance still came above and beyond everything else.

Over the next month or so, Sammy simmered down enough to tell me that if I finished with Corky, he would never mention it again, we could draw a line under the whole thing and dance the World Championship together, a competition we'd both been building to our whole lives.

Around the same time, Corky gave me an ultimatum. He said it was over between us if I danced the World Championship with Sammy.

It was the most stomach-churning decision I've ever had to make, but in the end I went with my heart and ran into the arms of Corky, pulling out of the championships and calling time on the Non-stop Stopfords.

I suppose I was searching for something more than what I already had.

A year after first meeting him in Quebec, I gave up everything for Corky and moved to Houston to start a new life thousands of miles away from home. Looking back, what we had together was an incredibly intense, red-blooded love affair. I had fallen head over heels for him, which completely clouded my better judgement.

And from his point of view, he was desperate to be a professional dancer and liked what I could offer in that regard.

This is just my gut talking and I've never asked him the question outright, but I almost feel like Corky didn't really have any choice but to marry me. I'd made huge sacrifices to be with him and so, under pressure from his father George, we were wed in September 1985. Our baby boy Mark was born the following May.

I will always be thankful for our relationship as we both got a beautiful son out of it. I guess we got one thing right.

It was explosive right from the off and our marriage was characterised by rows, betrayals and power struggles. I honestly couldn't tell you how we managed to cling on as long as we did. I dare say it was for the sake of Mark, whom we both doted on.

In the beginning, Corky and I loved each other immensely, but we were on that hamster wheel and the love went out of the window. I certainly put the walls up, as did he, and I know I soon felt defensive, miserable and insecure.

I never possessed the right communication skills to make the relationship work. I was so young when we got together; we had a baby; we were travelling; we moved to England … there were so many moving parts and eventually we couldn't make any of them fit. We tried to get it back, but we weren't ever in sync. When I wanted to get back together, he didn't and vice versa.

The inevitable divorce was as bitter as it possibly could be and I was left reeling from the fallout and having to rebuild my life. Some of the best advice I ever gave to my son was not to get married until he was at least 30.

'You do your thing first,' I said, 'and settle down after that.'

He took that advice on board and married BC Jean, a fabulous American singer-songwriter, when he was in his early thirties and I've never met a man more in love with a woman or seen a couple more compatible. They are like peas in a pod and the two of them have everything in a relationship I wished I could have had myself.

> 'Sometimes it takes a heartbreak to shake us awake and help us see we are worth so much more than we're settling for.'
>
> MANDY HALE

In my experience, relationships form and then they fizzle. The forming part is great fun – that's the honeymoon phase where the physical attraction is at its peak and you're blimmin' nuts about each other.

The fizzle? I don't like that one bit – I keep moving forward but boy do I feel heartbreak. It's a searing, physical pain which cuts me deep and then leaves me hollow.

After being on my own for a while, I enjoyed two long-term relationships, one after the other and both with younger men who were dancers. I guess I was lucky that they were kind people and we had some happy times, but they proved hard relationships to break from.

The first was an extremely talented dancer and I was besotted with him. We lived, travelled, taught and sometimes performed together, I met his family in Italy who were all wonderful, and after the heartache of my marriage split, he made me feel alive again.

I didn't ever look too far into the future, but I was totally committed to him and certainly never saw myself being with anyone else. We were together for many years until he told me he'd fallen in love with his dance partner, a stunning blonde Russian who had been one of my very best students for a long time. That was it for me.

I should have seen it coming, really. The two of them went on to become ten times world champions together (and would also eventually marry) and I suppose they found their destiny.

I've never spoken about this in depth publicly before because it was always too painful. The hurt lasted a long time afterwards and there were a lot of tears shed as I tried to make sense of losing someone I cared so deeply about.

I went on to have a few dates with some perfect gentlemen, but really I was still picking up the pieces when I found my next boyfriend.

He shared my drive, he made me laugh and I found the way he cared for other people, especially his parents back home in Russia, completely charming.

I know people were sniggering about me choosing someone else in the industry. One person charmingly said, 'Well, you should just enjoy the intimacy, because it's never going to last.'

They didn't realise that we actually had a lot in common and learned so much from each other. I went to Russia and met his parents – he's got the most fantastic family, a mum and dad who couldn't be nicer.

Did it last? No. And I had my heart broken again. But the years I spent with him were some of the best times. Of course, there was gossip and judgement aplenty about my so-called 'toyboys' but I was used to that. I'd spent my life being judged, right from the playground and all the way to professionally as a dancer.

Judgement doesn't faze me.

But again, a relationship formed then it fizzled. Over our six years together, infidelity came into play and gradually the trust ebbed away until it was gone completely. Once you've lost that, there's no coming back.

After the split, I took my mum to Hawaii on a cruise – this boyfriend had been due to join us so my friend Terrie travelled in his place. I was devastated and crying every day, sitting in the bar sobbing into my daiquiri.

One evening my mum had clearly had enough of my 'wah-wah-wah' and gave me a thoroughly good telling-off.

'Get over it, Shirley!' she said, storming away from the table. 'I'm not going to listen to this my whole holiday.'

I was rendered speechless from the sheer shock of my mother's outburst. But you know what? I got my act together for the rest of the trip.

Sometimes it takes a bolt from the blue (or a smack in the chops) to snap you out of your pity party. My mum has no time for wallowers, she's a product of a tough life herself.

I'll give one of those ex-boyfriends his due because he was later offered a large sum of money to sell his story about me, which he declined. He said everything would stay between him and me, which is exactly as it should be. We've remained friends and I still teach him with his wife. He's a good soul.

Sometimes people come into your life but aren't necessarily meant to stay and I like to think our paths crossed when they did for a reason.

Nevertheless, the breakups left me devastated, single again and contemplating if I wasn't destined to be alone.

'Sometimes good things fall apart so better things can fall together.'

MARILYN MONROE

Danny Taylor was the first person I ever felt truly cared about the human side of me and when we met doing pantomime together in 2018, I thought I'd finally met my Mr Right. I'd been single for nearly three years by then and was searching for company and affection.

God, I loved the mortal bones of that man and even after several years together, I always got excited when I saw him. Butterflies.

I think I fell for Danny far sooner than he did me. He thought we were just a panto romance which would peter out in the New Year, but I wanted something more serious and long term. After the panto run finished, he went straight on tour with *Blood Brothers*, playing Sammy, one of the lead roles, and I'd join him at certain locations. By March 2019, we realised we had developed deep feelings for each other.

I fell in love with the way he looked after people. I watched him with his mother and his family and I was drawn to him because I'd never seen a man behave so tenderly and with such compassion.

He made me feel beautiful, valued and appreciated. I used to go to bed with my makeup on, a habit from past relationships where there had been pressure to look immaculate at all times. One night Danny gently asked why I did that and then told me I didn't have to be anybody but myself with him.

I removed all the makeup and my lashes and he said, 'Now, there she is.'

He was tall, dark and handsome and a good cuddler. He was kind, never pushy or demanding and he gave me my confidence back. But unfortunately, there was another side to Danny, as there is with everybody, and there were challenges.

Danny and I both had complicated backgrounds which we bonded over and while I do believe he loved me, there were always fragilities in the relationship, cracks beneath the surface that became gaping crevices when everything started imploding.

Danny's a drifter by nature and I began to feel like Nelly the nagger. If we ever had a row or even a discussion that became slightly heated, we'd end up not communicating for days on end, which reminded me of what my dad used to do when he'd go to the corner shop for a pint of milk and disappear off the face of the planet for the next six weeks.

The things I used to laugh at and find endearing in Danny – if he was coming to stay with me in London, I'd never know what time his train was getting in, or he'd arrive at my front door with a suitcase in disarray – started to grate. And the more I thought about these quirks of character, the more I realised that they weren't actually funny. Alarm bells started ringing.

Lust dwindles. After that, you want intelligence, drive, somebody who pulls their weight, a friend, loyalty, fun. Sometimes you can be with a person you adore and yet want more for yourself and it was slowly dawning on me that I needed someone in my life who was going to move forwards with me, so we could do better and benefit together.

I adored Danny and showered him with gifts, thinking that's how I should show him I loved him. He had the best of the best – tailor-made clothes, Gucci shoes, Mont Blanc cufflinks, gorgeous holidays, a Mini Coupé. During Covid when everyone in the acting industry was struggling, I hired him as my PA because I felt bad that he wasn't able to earn a living.

I think I was having doubts about the future for a whole year before it ended for good, but I hadn't been ready to let go. Maybe it was always going to take a shocking event to force me into making that break and eventually Danny put me in a position where I had no choice.

The nail in the coffin came on 6 September 2024. It was my 64th birthday and I'd been out for a lovely lunch with my mum in London. Danny was back home in Liverpool.

That evening, my mother and I had snuggled up in her bed chatting about what a nice day we'd had when at about 9pm, my phone rang. It was a family member of Danny's and I sensed something wasn't right as I answered. They told me they couldn't locate him, he'd switched his phone off and he'd left a worrying note, which immediately took my mind back to my brother.

The family member asked if they could pass on my number to the police, who then explained the seriousness of the note. My heart sank. I felt just like I did when I lost my brother back in 2003. My mother and I were up all night frantically trying to track Danny down. I called his friends and his family and just couldn't sleep. At 2am, I noticed my WhatsApps to Danny had two blue ticks next to them, indicating he'd read them, and there was also a 'last seen' notification at the top of the chat screen, which strongly suggested he had turned his mobile on and viewed the messages.

The next day Danny reappeared and tried to act like nothing had happened. A friend of his had reassured me that this would happen, as it wasn't the first time he had done this.

I had been up throughout the night with my mother, beside ourselves with worry and reliving all the trauma we'd suffered with my brother. I knew then that I couldn't have someone in my life who was capable of putting me through that time and time again.

I called Danny and asked to meet with him so we could sit down and talk like grown-ups – you already know how I prefer to do things face to face. We never did get the chance to sit down with each other, which is a shame as he'll always have a special place in my heart and I don't like anything to end on bad terms.

The majority of the people who pass through my life I stay in touch with because I make it that way. My mother is the opposite – cross her and you're out!

Danny and I haven't seen each other since we broke up. I've written him many messages but haven't often heard back. Perhaps he doesn't realise the mark he's left on me. I'd wanted to marry him at one stage; I had bought the engagement and wedding rings, we loved each other's company and we laughed a lot.

But even though I tried my very best, it reached a point where I had to step away. I can't wear someone else's problems for the rest of my life.

And I don't want to sound like a person who doesn't care, because I do. Deeply. But I've learned that after a certain point I can't be responsible for other people's troubles. I could guide Danny to the right support and offer advice, but I've also got to recognise when it's time and sometimes you have to remove yourself because the situation becomes detrimental to your own health.

There were lots of good times, but not enough to outweigh the bad, and that's an imbalance I don't want to bear the brunt of as I head into my twilight years. Not to be morbid, but when 'the end' is drawing near, I don't want my time to be a test of endurance.

I'd rather be single than that.

Now that everything is calmer, I feel relieved to be free and, weirdly, the heartbreak somehow felt a little easier than with previous partners because the relationship had distanced over such a long period of time. It wasn't as sudden and shocking.

My door is always open if Danny wants to talk and I'd love to see if we can salvage a friendship. In the meantime, I've been getting used to being on my own again, which hasn't been easy. I feel incomplete and a little lost.

But I can only tolerate people's nonsense for so long. Then one day I will blow. Imagine filling a suitcase with junk, stuffing more and more into it, then trying to zip it shut, stretching the seams. Eventually, that zip is going to give and the whole thing will burst open.

That's me.

I make the decision and there's no turning back.

'Sometimes, those who fly solo have the strongest wings.'

ANONYMOUS

I won't marry again, I can tell you that now. Been there, done that, too many disasters to my name. Call me a cynic, but I struggle to believe that anything is forever.

I have a mother, not a lover, because she's the only one who will put up with me!

I do miss having someone to go out with, though. I miss the closeness and the affection and the little squeezes. I miss companionship and having that special someone who says, 'OK, get ready. We're going out …' I miss having nice things to look forward to with somebody and sharing the peaks and troughs of my day.

I worry about when I'm older, who's going to keep me company? Who's going to take care of me?

I get lonely. Mind you, I can be in the most crowded room and still feel lonely. There's no reason why I should – I'm surrounded by dancers all day long, I'm constantly on the phone talking about dresses to be made, competitions to be entered, *Strictly* this, *Strictly* that … always something going on.

And yet.

I may no longer have faith in love, but I still have desire and passion. In the dance industry, I'm constantly surrounded by couples – I teach them, work with them and judge alongside them and so I can't help but think it would be nice to have someone special again.

My body's growing old, my hair's going grey, the skin wrinkles and everything starts sagging and bagging, but the heart stays the same. You still want somebody to look at you and think, 'Oh, you look nice.'

With all of that in mind, I have thought about joining the exclusive member-only dating app Raya, known for catering to people with public profiles or who are high up in the world of business.

I'm a bit nervous about signing up, but who cares in this day and age? My wishlist of preferences isn't particularly extensive; I'm realistic and I don't expect the moon on a stick. But I do like a handsome man with a good personality and a kind heart – they have to take care of themselves and those around them.

The age bracket I've gone for is fairly broad but not too young – I think my 'toyboy' days are behind me. I reckon anything from 55 to 70 if they're fit. Up to 98 if they're loaded!

Just joking.

They have to be completely unattached – I don't do married men because that's been done to me and I'd never put another woman through that same hurt. I'd also like them to be financially independent and able to take me to dinner once in a while.

I don't think that's too much to ask for, do you?

I'm quite proud of myself for dipping my toe into a modern dating world I know so little about. Years ago, when I lived in the States, I went on a date through Match.com and I'd not long before read a story about a dismembered head that had been found in a bin, which made me ever so slightly nervous. So I told my gay gaggle Alan and Nathan to book into the same restaurant incognito so they could keep an eye on me.

The guy I was meeting was an artist from Switzerland, and it turned out to be the longest three hours of my life listening to him drone on about his flipping brush strokes. It was all I could do to keep myself awake and by the time he'd finished talking I'd lost the will to live, quite frankly.

That was enough for me and I've never been back to online dating since.

But let's see what Raya brings. They say that when you find love later in life you do it with all the wisdom of knowing heartbreak and all the peace of knowing who you are. I like that sentiment, but I'm asking all the single women in their sixties, how much of a market is there for us?

And while I'm very open to having a date, I'm very much *not* open to anyone's slippers under my counter. Keep your dressing gown and your slippers in your own house, thanks all the same – I don't want to live with a man again.

Anyone coming into my life at this stage would have to understand how busy and complicated my schedule is and that I'm up at 6am, often at work by seven, regularly head off to America to visit family and if I ever have a day off, I take my mum out, I walk the dog, I see friends and I like to pop to Marks & Spencer.

I hardly have time for myself, let alone anyone else.

I struggle to imagine having a full-time relationship with someone who isn't in the same industry as me because they'll never grasp what it's all about.

There are advantages to not being attached and there is plenty I enjoy about single life. I like going to bed at night without having to deal with any drama on the end of the phone.

There's a lot to be said for having the freedom to get up and go wherever I like without having to answer to anyone. I get a lot of pleasure from having a handsome bloke on my arm, but at my age it's not worth the heartache if that's what he's bringing with him.

There might be somebody out there, you never know, but I don't think love and marriage were ever my destiny.

My mother never remarried after my dad. She's had a few boyfriends along the way, but she's stayed on her own and always been perfectly happy that way.

I'm happy too. Happy for me is when the phone rings and I see it's Mark calling. It's when I see my grandson. Happiness is when I'm laughing with my mum around the dinner table.

Perhaps I'm learning that I don't need a man to complete me.

Shirley's Shimmers

If you're heartbroken over a breakup,
remember they lost you, not the other way around.

✗

People will come and go from your life but them
leaving does not signal the end of your story.
It's just the end of their part in your story.

✗

Love should feel safe, not like a rollercoaster
— couples should grow together and nurture
each other, not hold each other back.

✗

No drama, no games — you deserve peace
and happiness and knowing where you stand.

✗

The right person adds to your life;
they do not become it or take away from it.

✗

Make a life so good for yourself that you
don't need someone else to complete it.

✗

You are whole on your own.

STEP FIVE

Learn to Pivot

REDIRECTION

'You can't go back and start a new beginning, Shirley. But you can write a new ending.'

AUDREY

I love the word 'pivot'. In dance it's a turning foot, rotating to change direction, creating a fluid movement that flows into the next step. Depending on the style of dance, the pivot can be small and controlled or dramatic and dynamic.

Life can be like that, too.

Sometimes we have no choice but to pivot and change course. I've come to many a fork in the road (and a fair few dead ends, too) – times when I've had to make a crucial decision, turn on my heel and shift.

As my gay gaggle would say, 'Ball, change.'

But I've always believed that when life gives you lemons, you make lemonade. In other words, if things go belly up, you turn that negativity into positivity.

Back in 2016, when I was in the pits of despair about the concerted attempts to destroy my teaching career by those hell-bent on making sure none of the world's top dancers would touch me with a bargepole, my mother (who, as you probably know by now, doesn't do tea and sympathy and has zero time for moping) said, 'That's just your ego talking, Shirley.'

She asked me if it really mattered who I taught.

Did I need to be teaching the top professionals and world champions when the younger generations needed coaching too?

After all, I could teach beginners, juveniles or juniors from four years old, or I could even go into the world of pro-am, which is a bit like *Strictly* in that you pair a professional with an amateur.

I had options, I just had to make that swivel, refocus and reroute. I was actually in a position of great strength because from the age of 17 I'd put in the hard yards and made sure I was the most qualified I could possibly be in my profession and in all dance teacher societies. I'd taken all my technical exams in every area of dance and was therefore eligible to teach and examine at any level, from a small child to champion.

Today I'm a Fellow, qualified at the highest level in the global Imperial Society of Teachers of Dance, where I'm also the President.

As per usual my mother was completely right. I wiped away my tears, put those big girl pants on and started all over again, teaching anyone who wanted me. I'd sometimes be with my little beginners while my friends were teaching a class of pros in the same studio and I'll be honest, it made me boil with rage at the bullies who had tried to break me.

But the best form of revenge is to crack on and keep moving down the bus.

I did more than that. I hit the accelerator, rebuilt my business and regained my sense of worth. And, to my surprise, I found it a real joy to teach such a wide variety of students across the spectrum of abilities – it was dance that I loved, not the kudos. And that's the thing about being forced to make a change, it can sometimes lead to happiness when you're least expecting it. It might not have been where I'd seen myself heading, but I'd taken back control of my life and career.

We can't direct the wind, but we can adjust the sails … and I was the captain of my own ship.

> 'Every change is a
> challenge to become
> who we really are.'
>
> ANONYMOUS

I'm a roll the dice kind of woman. I know a lot of people get apprehensive about change and risk, but I relish taking that leap of faith and trying something new.

I've been like that forever: as a dance competitor, I'd always want to try something daring, incorporating a step that nobody else would even attempt. It's why I've moved house so many times without a blink. Up, down, pack your bags and leave – I'm not attached to material possessions or bricks and mortar. You can only pee on one toilet, sleep in one bed and wear one set of clothes – that's another Audrey-ism. I've gone through every phase in life, from super rich to super skint and what I have learned about money is that it can give you a good lifestyle, but it sure as hell doesn't make you happy. I know a lot of very wealthy people who are miserable as sin and a lot of poor people who are some of the happiest souls I've ever come across.

Probably the craziest dice roll I ever made was to take on the seemingly impossible task of turning Corky Ballas into a world champion dancer. When I look back now, I realise what a challenge that was and think I must have been stark raving mad.

Corky was a decent pro-amateur who was desperate to become a professional – he was small in stature but towering with ambition and already thought he was the world's greatest dancer before we had even set foot on the floor as a couple, it was just that he hadn't yet been discovered.

After I moved to Houston to be with him in 1984, I was in demand as a pro-am teacher and earning good money, but I longed to return to competitive dance. I'd given everything up without really considering how much I would miss being at the heart of the industry I adored and so, against my better judgement, I came up with the idea of training Corky to be my new partner.

To say the plan was a bold one would be an understatement. Bloody crackers would be more accurate because I didn't just want us to be good enough to compete, I wanted us to be crowned ultimate champions. That meant we had a steep road ahead of us.

I'll say it exactly how it was: Corky was an almighty pain in the arse to teach. He'll admit that himself – he was the most difficult and obstinate person I've ever taught. He was a pro-am dancer but thought he knew it all and he had a self-belief that was off the scale and beyond anything I'd ever witnessed.

He also had a work ethic to match my own and the skin of a rhino – for all his shortcomings, he is the human embodiment of tenacity and is actually the perfect example of being able to get to wherever you want to go, as long as you set your mind to it.

Snake-hipped and physically strong, he *looked* like a dancer, so we had some pretty good foundations to build on. He was also rather good-looking. That helped.

Nevertheless, it was humbling for me starting at the bottom with an unknown having been British Open to the World champion with Sammy just a year before. Nobody, and I mean nobody, believed we could do it and I know plenty were laughing up their sleeves as the word spread. We were the butt of everybody's jokes.

Not many were willing to help us, either. That's another typical trait of dance: everybody wants to be on your team if you're successful, but the minute that you're not, they'll chuck you away like a piece of rubbish. With a few notable exceptions, most will ignore you if you're no longer at the top of your game.

A few old contacts were willing to help – Nina Hunt flew over to teach us, as did former world champions Alan and Hazel Fletcher, Robert and Helen Ritchey and even Sammy Stopford, who showed great magnanimity when he offered us a lesson while he was on tour in the States. I'm so glad we managed to remain friends, as we are to this day.

Putting up with Corky's often outrageous behaviour in the studio – not to mention his foul mouth – put me through my paces and gave me some of my toughest days in dance. But we had a shared goal that neither one of us took our eyes off and we both knew we needed each other to get there.

We were never going to give in and, against all the odds, Corky and I went on to win the United States Closed Championships in 1986, months after I'd given birth to our son Mark. It was a title we won multiple times over the subsequent years and, I have to hand it to Corky, it's a major achievement which should not be downplayed. For someone to have gone from the pro-am circuit to United States professional champ was unprecedented and historic.

To have done it in such a short space of time was ridiculous.

Corky has since grudgingly acknowledged that I was a good teacher and says now that he would never have won without me being there for him.

We pivoted again after moving back to the UK in 1990 with the intention of having one last shot at hitting the big time. It was going to be another gargantuan challenge, and we were starting at the bottom of the ladder again in more ways than one.

Corky's family, who'd had more money than you'd know what to do with in ten lifetimes, had suffered a series of cataclysmic financial misfortunes and we'd had to give up our luxury lifestyle.

Back in Texas, we'd both driven a Mercedes Benz, had access to limousines and helicopters and we'd lived in a beautiful house in Katy, just west of Houston – and now we were moving into a poky two-up, two-down in one of the not so salubrious areas of London. This place had bugs on the carpet and a leak in the ceiling and I remember asking the landlord if it was OK for us to paint the walls at least.

'Yes,' he said, 'go ahead.'

We decorated that house from top to bottom and as soon as we'd finished, the landlord sold it and kicked us out. As a family, we moved around between flats and houses depending on how well we were doing financially – having no money was fine for me because I'd been there before and got the T-shirt, but it was an alien concept to Corky who, to his credit, rolled up his sleeves and got on with it.

Together we moved mountains.

Under the expert guidance of some fantastic teachers, including Ruud Vermeij, a competitive dancer turned professor with a doctoral degree in ballroom dancing who had also studied psychotherapy, we clawed our way up the rankings.

In 1995 we found ourselves in the final of the British championships at the Winter Gardens in Blackpool, the same title I'd won with Sammy 12 years earlier.

As fate would have it, we were up against Sammy Stopford and his partner Barbara McColl, who were number one at the time. We'd never *ever* beaten them before. Although Sammy and Barbara won the Rumba, Corky and I took the Cha-Cha-Cha, the Samba, Paso Doble and the Jive to be crowned British Open to the World Latin champions. It was against all the odds, and something nobody thought was possible for us. We made the impossible bloody possible. Incredible.

When it was announced we'd won, Corky ran onto the dance floor and, in a moment of pure insanity, did a backflip and landed flat on his back. It must have hurt like crazy but he was too ecstatic to notice. That said it all.

He had silenced his critics and achieved something that every single person, including my own mother, had said was impossible.

We claimed the same title again the following year, before retiring having proved everyone wrong. No one can ever take that away from us and even all these years later, part of me still doesn't quite believe that we pulled it off.

But mastering the art of the pivot is about so much more than reacting to change. It's about having a steely determination to make sure the alternative route is a fruitful one and leads to something even greater than before.

'You are never too old to set another goal or to dream a new dream.'

LES BROWN

It doesn't matter what town, city or country I've been in, I've never worried about finding work. Word travels fast in dance and if you put it about that you're available, the phone starts ringing almost immediately. And for that I always feel truly blessed.

But even if I didn't have that buffer, I'm a go-getter and don't really care what I have to do to earn my keep. I'd be happy enough cleaning loos as long as I was bringing in a wage.

While I was living in the States after following Mark and Derek over there in 2007, other opportunities besides teaching started cropping up too. *Dancing with the Stars* had a spin-off show called *AfterBuzz*, a bit like the BBC's *It Takes Two*, and I made a few quite fun appearances on there. During one of the seasons they put together a feature about an industry icon and chose me as the subject.

Well, I was chuffed to pieces.

I enjoyed being in and around the fizz of a TV studio and I started to wonder … I was spending hours upon hours every day teaching and travelling around the world to judge competitions and had begun to feel a little restless with it all. Was there something else out there for me? Was I capable of something more?

Did I have another pivot in me?

It was my son who had first heard an industry whisper that the legendary Len Goodman was leaving *Strictly Come Dancing* and he suggested I put a call in. I'd known Len for a long time because we'd lived close to each other in London and he'd trained Corky and me on and off over a number of years. But TV wasn't my natural habitat and I didn't even have an agent so assumed the job would be way out of my league anyway, even if the rumours were true.

I actually already had contacts on the show because now and again they'd ask me if I could recommend any professionals to potentially join the cast, something I'd always been happy to help with.

As it happened, in the autumn of 2016 the team were having a look at one of my couples, so we arranged to meet for a coffee and a chat when I was back in the UK to teach ahead of the International Championships. By now, Len had confirmed that this current series of *Strictly* would indeed be his last – he also judged on *Dancing with the Stars* and the transatlantic commuting had become too exhausting.

I met the producers at a restaurant and although the topic of Len's departure and his replacement didn't come up, I do remember the conversation veered off into dance technique, which always gets me quite animated (in a good way!). Maybe that triggered something with the Beeb. After that meeting I returned to the States to continue my usual life of teaching and coaching, until one day my son asked why I didn't try out for the job. I decided to throw caution to the wind – I had nothing to lose.

Well, the stars all seemed to align, which is how I found myself returning to the UK at my own expense to audition, not really knowing what to expect and not daring to get any hopes up either.

I didn't tell a soul and asked the *Strictly* team not to publicise it unless I was offered the job, a prospect I thought highly unlikely considering my lack of telly experience and the fact I was an unknown outside of the dance world.

Let alone that I was pushing 60.

I flew in from LA on the Thursday and headed straight to the audition, thinking I had nothing to lose and imagining I was one of several people they were seeing. If you'd believed the buzz around all the dance circles, the world and his wife were up for this, the hottest job vacancy in town.

I've spoken before about how that try-out wasn't my finest hour. My sciatica was giving me trouble, I was jet lagged and all that made it difficult for me to relax during the screen test. There is something very daunting about sitting there looking down the barrel of a camera lens with what feels like a thousand lights in your face and lots of people all there to assess your performance.

There's no point in pretending otherwise – I performed dreadfully, it was an awful experience and I left the building believing I'd blown it.

I phoned Mark and told him how badly it had gone and that I hadn't felt good enough to be there.

He listened, but he didn't sit there and commiserate with me and he wasn't going to allow me to feel sorry for myself or lick my wounds. Not on your nelly.

Instead, he said this was a job I'd been training for my whole life, albeit unwittingly. I had earned my stripes and had more than enough credentials to sit on that panel, I just needed to get over the nerves and be myself.

He said the down-to-earth working-class grit that runs through my DNA was what people watching would relate to and that if I was given a callback, I had to grab it with both hands.

Not long after my pep talk from Mark, I got a call from the executive producer Louise Rainbow, who asked me how I thought I'd done. I was completely honest with her and said I was frustrated with myself that I'd allowed the jitters to get the better of me and how much I wished I could rewind and start again.

I was due to fly back to LA the next day, but Louise said if I was able to change my flight, I was very welcome to come back and have another go. Talk about a second chance! You don't look gift horses like that in the mouth, so I rebooked my flight and returned to the audition studio the following day in a very different frame of mind. Reminding myself of that conversation with Mark and his advice just to be me, I was much more relaxed and when I left that second audition, I was happy that I'd given it my very best shot.

What will be, I thought, will be.

'Embrace failure. Missteps and roadblocks are inevitable but are ultimately an opportunity to learn, pivot, and go after your goals with new perspective.'

JENNIFER FLEISS

A pivot doesn't always have to arise out of necessity. Sometimes opportunities offer the chance of an exciting reinvention and I'm living proof that it's never too late to make a switch. It still requires courage to face it and embrace it, but the biggest mistake we can make is not taking a chance in the first place.

Everybody was up in arms when I got the *Strictly* job. It sent the dance world into a frenzy and I think people were quite stunned by the announcement. Myself included!

Women aged 57 with zero TV experience don't get given plum roles on flagship TV shows. I'd done the odd appearance on *AfterBuzz* but never mind next level, this job was on another planet.

Thank God Louise Rainbow gave me that second opportunity, something I'll always be grateful to her for. She obviously saw something in me that no one else did, least of all myself.

I think she recognised a hard worker who was willing to learn. Someone with a vulnerability which would resonate with viewers. I hadn't breezed in there giving it the big I Am, and in our call after the first audition I'd held my hands up to what had gone wrong and then come back the next day determined to put it right.

'Give me an opportunity,' I'd said to her, 'and I'll make you proud.'

I hope I've done that. This year will be my ninth series and I learn something new each year and from every contestant and professional who graces that floor.

I've met so many inspiring people through the show – none more so than Chris McCausland who won in 2024 and Rose Ayling-Ellis who won in 2021. Blind and deaf respectively, they not only challenged preconceived notions about disability and dance, but they also captured the true spirit of *Strictly* and showed the world the meaning of determination.

Rose and her partner Giovanni Pernice's Couple's Choice dance to Clean Bandit's 'Symphony' where the music cut in the middle, plunging the studio into silence to give a glimpse into Rose's world, was one of the most spectacular performances I've ever witnessed.

Chris and his partner Dianne Buswell did something similarly poignant and thought-provoking with their Couple's Choice to John Lennon's 'Instant Karma!', turning the studio lights off halfway through, so we all had a few seconds of Chris's perspective.

Ashley Roberts was another one that will live long in the memory – she danced in tribute to her late father in 2018. Bobby Brazier's 2023 performance for his mum Jade Goody and Pete Wicks dedicating his Couple's Choice dance to his grandmother in 2024 also both moved me to tears.

I've watched people who have been going through difficult times in their lives come on the show and blossom. Annabel Croft was dealing with the sudden loss of her husband in 2023 and she danced through her grief. There wasn't a dry eye in the house during her American Smooth with Johannes Radebe, performed in Blackpool to 'Unchained Melody'.

TV presenter Helen Skelton was coping with a very public marriage split in 2022 and we saw her grow in confidence throughout the series, going on a journey which included her outstanding Couples Choice in the quarter–final, dubbed her 'revenge dance'. She later described her *Strictly* experience as 'liberating' – and it showed.

I also adore watching the beautiful friendships develop from the dance-floor partnerships. Ellie Leach and Vito Coppola in 2023 were particularly gorgeous and it's lovely when they form these lifelong connections because the show is built around unity.

There have also been people like Kelvin Fletcher who, with no dance experience whatsoever, won with Oti Mabuse in 2019, and those types of contestants continue to astound me in the best possible way.

And then there's Ann Widdecombe, who was before my time on the show but is a woman I have always admired for how she completely and utterly embraced the *Strictly* experience with her partner, Anton Du Beke.

'If you think that dance was bad, wait till you see what we've got for next week,' she'd say.

I loved the way that she won the hearts of the viewers and had the audience in the palm of her hand, even those who vehemently disagreed with her politics. It was a masterclass.

The *Strictly* success story is unparalleled. In an age where the way people watch TV is light years from how they did when the show began back in 2004, we're still pulling in ten million viewers every Saturday night, which is incredible after 20 years.

Long may it reign.

I am insanely lucky to be part of it. I feel especially honoured to be part of something which has been so pioneering for women in TV, with two female presenters at the helm, and myself and Motsi sitting on the panel alongside the great Craig and Anton.

Strictly has opened many doors for me, but I don't think I ever saw it as a reinvention. It was more a fresh challenge at a time when I needed it and had been looking to get my teeth into something new.

Having almost lost everything I'd worked for in 2016, it was also a vindication.

I was back to where I was before.

> 'You are braver than you believe,
> stronger than you seem, and
> smarter than you think.'
>
> A.A. MILNE

In all my years as the Queen of Latin, dancing my way up the ranks to become British Open to the World Latin champion, I've never worked harder than in pantomime.

It's tremendous fun but dear God, the graft is real and I was so stressed by it I struggled to remember my own name, let alone all my lines.

I was approached for panto after my first season on *Strictly*, one of many doors that were suddenly popping up for me to push open. It was to play Mother Nature in *Jack and the Beanstalk* at the Liverpool Empire – a homecoming for me – and my agent somehow managed to convince me I could do it.

I'd never been on the stage and didn't have a clue how to act, but I accepted the job on the condition that they gave me the script several months in advance so that I'd have plenty of time to learn my lines. Most panto casts don't start rehearsals until November, yet here I was practising my part (over and over and over) from May.

With all that preparation time, you'd be forgiven for assuming that I'd have it nailed by winter, but over the months I managed to develop a kind of weird dependency on the script itself to the point where I physically couldn't put it down. I was like a toddler with a security blanket and in the end the excellent director Bob Tomson had to pretty much prise it out of my trembling hands.

I remember going to see him privately, crying that I'd bitten off way more than I could chew and would not be able to see this through.

Bob sat there and listened to me pour my heart out and then he said, 'Well, my dear, you've signed a contract so you have absolutely no choice, I'm afraid. If I was you, I'd just get on with it.'

That was exactly the sort of kick up the arse my mother would have given me and, of course, Bob was absolutely right to do so, although my stress levels didn't dip much below 100 for the entire run. Even backstage before I went on, I'd be poring over the script, petrified that I was going to forget one of my lines.

As is so often the way, my taking a punt and doing that first panto proved to be fateful because it's where I met and fell in love with Danny. Funny how a single decision can end up shaping your whole future.

Danny was playing Fleshcreep, the Giant's evil henchman, and we became good friends – he was so generous with his time and spent hours going over my lines with me. He was also my real-life hero, rescuing me on a few occasions where I cocked it up on stage. In one of the very early shows, I somehow managed to skip two pages of script, but Danny effortlessly moved on and covered for me so I didn't look like an idiot. He knew that script inside and out so if I ever missed a line, he would rescue it without even flinching. I loved that about him.

I went on to do panto for a few years running, but I've decided to hang up my fairy wings for now. It's such a huge commitment over the festive period and while my mum's still with us I want to enjoy every minute of the Christmases we have remaining together.

But I'd surprised myself. You miss 100 per cent of the shots you don't take and by stepping outside of my comfort zone, I'd found new confidence.

Mind you, that doesn't mean I started saying 'yes' to everything. There are certain opportunities I know for a fact *are* beyond me and I've turned them down without a second thought. I've been asked to do *Celebrity Mastermind* and *Who Wants to be a Millionaire?* and I've always said 'thanks, but no thanks' because I'm hopeless at quizzes. Having said that, I am always open to changing my mind.

I know I'm an advocate of not fearing failure; however, I draw the line at having a total brain freeze in front of a chortling nation.

But I'm always open to ideas and learning new skills, which is why I work so well with Vito Coppola for our new business venture, Dance With Us. It's something I'd had a vision of for many years, as I'm so passionate about getting the country dancing and showing people that anyone can feel joy from movement. It doesn't matter if you think you have two left feet or a tenuous relationship with rhythm, it's about getting up there and giving it a go, and I want to provide a comfortable space for people to do that. I want to get the dads dancing, to go into schools and old people's homes and break down those barriers, because dance should be for everyone.

I just needed someone to do it alongside, somebody with the right morals and who would follow my track. I found that in Vito – we're both Christians, both good people and we both want to give back to the community. I ran the idea past him and he was all in. It just works.

I can be quite strict, but he's very cuddly and open with no barriers at all, which makes for a good balance. I taught him when he was 13 so we've known each other for 20 years now – we've both come a long way since then!

Ours isn't a bog-standard dance class where customers have a little shake of the booty and go home again. With us it's an experience focused on making people feel good from the moment they walk in the door. Half an hour before the class starts, we meet everyone, have photographs taken and get to know people. They also get the opportunity for a Vito hug if they want one. Most do.

After that, we do a nice warm-up to 'Sweet Caroline', then I teach the class from a technical perspective and Vito from a freedom aspect. I give our novice dancers all the sorts of pointers I do on *Strictly*, so they all know their fregolinas from their fleckerls and by the end of the session, everyone can dance a little routine.

We don't want people learning something they'd never perform again so we encourage them to film Vito and I demonstrating the dance step by step, which means they can take a video lesson away with them and they've got it at home forever. At the end we have a Q&A session where they can ask me and Vito anything they want, within reason!

We have a lot of people that come in who are apprehensive. Many have never danced before so it can feel a little overwhelming for them at first and it's been wonderful bringing those people out of their shells – they go away feeling like they've achieved something, as well as having had an enjoyable morning or afternoon. We wanted it to feel like a Dance With Us family and we're building this lovely community of people who just want to dance and hear our stories.

I dance full on with Vito and we've got big plans for the brand – who knows, we might go international and on to a much bigger scale, offering something that's totally different to anything else out there. Travel with us. Dine with us. Live with us (actually, that might be pushing it!).

If you'd asked me a few years ago if I thought I'd be launching a new business in my mid-sixties I'd have said not a chance. But here we are and it feels like such a privilege.

I'd urge you, too, to see the changes of direction in your life – whether chosen or not – to be part of the process. Don't be frightened to have a go at something new; the only impossible journey is the one you never start.

Say yes!

You might be surprised where your pivot leads to.

Shirley's Shimmers

You can always turn a challenging situation round,
and sometimes adversity is the best driver for success.

✗

Pivoting is about growth and evolution –
each one can bring new, exciting opportunities.

✗

Be brave, be curious, be willing to tread new paths –
dare to dance in unfamiliar territory.

✗

Reframe the setbacks and see that every detour
can lead to something bigger and better.

✗

The best opportunities often come along
when you least expect them.

✗

Nothing has to be set in stone – you can
pivot again if you need to.

✗

Don't ask 'what if?' Instead ask 'why not?'

✗

Indecision only leads to stagnation.
Take a chance. Roll the dice.

STEP SIX

Master the Transitions

ADAPTABILITY

'You've got no choice,
so appreciate life
while you can.'

AUDREY

*T*ransitions in dance are the bridges between movements. They create a seamless flow, a gorgeous continuity – they are the glue that holds a routine together.

Our lives are full of transitions and if there's one thing I've learned from day dot, it's that nothing stays the same for long. I've moved house, cities and countries a whopping 28 times in total, so I've been readapting and readjusting ever since I was a little girl.

I go where my life takes me.

Sometimes I feel like I must be running away from something, I'm just not sure what. Like a lot of things, I haven't yet figured that one out.

But one thing I do know is that if we accept change as inevitable and understand that it will often take us out of our comfort zone, we can start to view those transitions as evolutions, approach them with a more open mind and find beauty in the journey.

It's all part of the process, isn't it? And you know, even the world's best dancers occasionally wobble through a transition.

Of all the transitional periods I've lived through, divorce has probably been the toughest and most profound because it forced me to redefine my identity, reconstruct my life from scratch and rethink my entire future. It took many years for the papers to come through with Corky because there was so much mudslinging and hurt and slagging backwards and forwards. It was ugly and when I look back now, I think, was that really necessary?

We had attempted marriage counselling and we'd tried to forgive each other for everything that had gone wrong in the relationship, but by the end it was obvious there was nothing to salvage. It didn't matter what I did, it was clear to me that I wasn't loved any more – there were times I felt that he couldn't even stand the sight of me – and I carry that rejection to this day.

I burrowed myself in my work, which has always been a safe place for me – stay on the treadmill, Shirley, just look ahead – but I had to sell our beautiful house in Dulwich as part of the settlement and start again. It wasn't long after losing my brother and it was like the deck of cards just fell.

My life had always been precariously balanced.

Divorce for me was a lonely place. Although it was the right decision to split, it was so much more than the end of a marriage; it was the unravelling of a whole life built up over two decades.

But they say rock bottom is sometimes the best foundation from which to start rebuilding. There was a time when I felt I couldn't be anything without Corky, but I proved myself wrong. Where there's a will there's a way, even when everything goes absolutely tits up.

I had to learn how to handle my finances as a single woman – Corky had always taken charge of the paperwork, the credit cards, phones, computers and anything money-related and hadn't ever let me get involved, so I was clueless on how to get a hold on things. My former dance partner Nigel Tiffany had been in and out of my life over a number of years and was a huge support, helping me to understand and take control of my money, which was key to me getting back on my feet.

It took what seemed like forever for me to grasp everything, but I did it and I've done it all on my own ever since.

Today my relationship with Corky is mostly on an even keel. We survived the divorce and emerged with a friendship of some description intact, but it's often been seriously tested – when I got the *Strictly* job, he gave an interview to the *Sun* which ruined things between us again for the best part of five years.

We're in a much better place now and I try to make the effort for the sake of Mark and our beautiful grandson Banksi, and I think Corky does too. He's still very stuck in his ways and his mouth is as foul as ever, but there is a softer, meeker side to him that not many people get to see.

I know it's there.

I didn't realise it until years after, but divorce made me stronger and wiser. Happier, too.

Life is nothing if not a series of changes and your future happiness hangs on whether you choose to mawkishly dwell on the past or take the bull by the horns and charge ahead.

The first is never an option for me.

'[Menopause] is a time of liberation. It's a time of shedding the shackles of inhibition and of giving a damn.'

DAVINA MCCALL

I was 50 years of age when my periods point-blank stopped. It wasn't a gradual tapering off as you might expect from around that time, they were literally here one month and gone the next.

It was at the time I'd just split with my boyfriend and I remember having my 50th birthday party while feeling wretched. Half a century on the planet, a time when you're supposed to be settled and sorted and yet here I was, crestfallen, on my own again and, although I didn't know it yet, about to embark on a menopause journey which would push me to the brink.

My mother never spoke to me about the menopause other than to say, 'Get on with it, Shirley.' She'd sailed through hers and at the time we had an ocean between us – I was in America and she was in England, so geography made it difficult to open up to her anyway.

It also simply wasn't talked about as it is now. It wasn't talked about at all! Sadly, I didn't have anybody in my circle I could discuss it with and I didn't know where to go for information. There wasn't the wealth of resources we have today.

Very quickly I started suffering with weight gain, night sweats, dry skin and hair loss. I'd get these hot flushes which came on with no warning and I'd burn from the neck up until my whole face was a bright red tomato. It was incredibly embarrassing. I was grumpy and extremely irritable, and my libido was shot. Sex became something I dreaded.

But the most debilitating change of all was to my mental health. I was anxious, depressed and desolate. I thought I was losing the plot. In my darkest hours I went to some terrible places in my head and while I hate to use the word suicidal, those thoughts crossed my mind.

I could never have gone through with it because I wouldn't want my mother to suffer the agony of losing a second child to suicide, but there were certainly times when I thought I'd be better off dead because the way I was living felt so hideous.

In true Shirley Ballas style, I'd always paint on a smile in front of other people and I remember having long conversations where I probably looked like I was engaged and interested, but I wasn't really listening. It was like being in a drum; everything was an echo. I was merely existing, working on autopilot and never fully present.

I'd always been such a jolly, positive, energetic person and suddenly I couldn't find that part of me. It was gone. I felt like a waste of space.

I used to pray that I'd wake up and be my old self again – I just wanted to feel happiness and to be OK enough to enjoy the day. I longed to be able to get up in the morning and feel like I could go about my daily duties and perform well, but I was dragging myself to work and teaching private lessons while this turmoil swirled inside of me.

I was grumpy and grouchy and could sometimes lash out at the people I was training. I had an attitude that I can see now might have come across as rude.

I'll never forget one day when I was teaching a couple from Dallas called Rangel Spirov and Veronika Chernyavska at the Westmor Dance Studio in LA and my mood was particularly sombre. I wasn't being the teacher that I could and should have been and Rangel took me to one side.

'I don't know what's going on in your life,' he said, 'but this is not you teaching us. I suggest you have a cup of coffee and come back to the lesson,' or words to that effect.

He was the first person who had ever done that, given me a stern talking-to about how my state of mind was affecting my work, and I shall be forever grateful to him because it shocked me into realising I needed to buck my ideas up and get some help.

For fear of being seen as weak, I was never the type to reach out or share my struggles. Instead I'd been trying to manage the 'situation' myself with antidepressants, sleeping tablets, more medication to wake myself up and, I have to say this, alcohol.

I'd always liked a social glass of wine with friends, but that was as far as it had gone. I was never a boozer or someone who would get anything beyond mildly tipsy. My mother was a party girl in her day and even now she likes a whisky and dry ginger, but that was never me.

However, now I was *drinking*. It had become a crutch which I thought was helping me to relax and unwind, something to take the edge off at the end of a busy day, but was actually making my anxiety even worse.

I'd get home from a day's teaching, lie on the bed feeling utterly dreadful for myself and open a bottle of red wine which I'd sink on my own. This was completely out of character for me and a sign of how far I'd fallen.

I knew it was becoming a problem. I'd developed a dependency on that evening bottle of red and I was doing all this in private, hiding the extent of my distress from my family and those around me. No one knew how difficult I was finding life and they were completely unaware of what was going on.

It was my son who realised first.

'OK, Mum,' he said, 'let's talk about where we can get you some help.'

We sat and talked for ages – I take my medicine very well from him.

Mark arranged for me to see the wonderful Dr Asandra in California, and when I sat down with him, everything about how I was feeling tumbled out at once. I told him about the uncontrollable physical symptoms, the drinking, the mood swings and how some days were so horrendous that I didn't want to live.

And Dr Asandra listened. He sat there so patiently as the tears rolled down my cheeks and then he gently told me that this was all to do with my hormones, which was news to me. It was the first time I'd considered that as a possible cause.

'Now this is what we're going to do,' he said, his whole tone so confident and reassuring, kind and caring. 'I'm going to give you some blood tests and we're going to sort this out.'

I felt a glimpse of hope and so began one of the most trans-formative chapters of my life.

The treatment was bioidentical hormone replacement ther-apy (BHRT) and involved a mini procedure where they make a small slice in the cheek of your bum and then implant a rice-sized pellet containing oestrogen and testosterone which drips into the bloodstream over a period of three to six months. He also put me on progesterone at night and then monitored me.

The change took several weeks, but over that time I felt a shift and began to feel like my old self again. Everything started to improve: my energy, my hair, skin, nails and mood. I felt mentally sharper, more emotionally balanced and physically stronger. And it wasn't long before the libido was back with a vengeance!

I was back in tune with my body, more present in my relationships and I rediscovered the confidence I'd lost long ago.

OK, here's where I make a confession. If I start to enjoy something, I'm one of those people who gets over-excited and wants more. I'm like a kid with candy. My regular GP in England had also prescribed oestrogen and testosterone in the form of a gel, which meant I was overloading on the stuff until I woke up one day with so much body hair 'Down There' you could weave a rug.

It had sprouted overnight!

I was coming out of the shower one morning and caught myself naked in the mirror and my jaw almost hit the floor.

'Good Lord!' I thought. 'Have mercy on us!'

My lady garden resembled a squirrel and required more than a quick trim. The garden shears might have been a better starting point.

Worst of all, and this is no word of a lie, I also now had a beard and a moustache, hairs coming out of my nose and ears and growing all over my toes. Eventually my dosage was tweaked and everything went back to normal, and these days I'll do a blood test every so often to make sure my levels remain good. I would like to think I'll be on HRT for the rest of my life, but it took me several years before I could say I was restored to full working order.

I'd say to every woman, please don't suffer in silence. I can't stress enough how important it is to get your hormones checked and I wish I'd asked for help sooner. We shouldn't have to settle for feeling anything less than whole and my experience is a powerful reminder that the right support can change everything.

For too long, men have been the gatekeepers of women's health and they are all too quick to dismiss us, not listen to us, assume they know best and to tell *us* how our bodies feel.

But it's we women who make the world go round. Without us, there would be none of them and because of that I believe we should be respected, treasured, taken care of and loved.

And given more bloody HRT than we can shake a stick at.

> *'It only takes one voice, at the right pitch, to start an avalanche.'*

DIANNA HARDY

It's a huge privilege to have a platform like mine, which is why I will always use it positively, and women's health is something I feel passionate about. Especially the specific areas we've been made to feel embarrassment over, the conditions that have traditionally been swept under the rug and become synonymous with shame.

Around the same time my HRT kicked in, I developed a condition called pruritus vulvae, which presents as an extremely uncomfortable and persistent itch in your intimate area.

Imagine being in a class with 500 people or going live on *Strictly* and having that come on all of a sudden … all you want to do is scratch, but you can't exactly do that discreetly in front of ten million viewers.

This time I haven't been too frightened or ashamed to ask for help and over the last seven years, I've been to the vulva clinic, I've seen doctors and have undergone a load of tests as they've tried to get to the bottom of what's causing it and find me appropriate treatment.

Years ago, I had a nervous disorder called urticaria, which made me itch all over my body and brought me out in rashes and hives. I'd been told it worked like a travelling caravan, starting at the fingertips, stopping at different parts of the body, moving to different destinations and causing mayhem. The doctor told me that one day the caravan would leave and never return, which is exactly what happened a few years after it started.

But if I thought the urticaria was bad, it was nothing compared to the pruritus vulvae. When it first started, it made me not want to leave the house, and I ended up taking time off work, which is unheard of for me.

I've recently been given amitriptyline, which is a mild anti-depressant and apparently sends a signal to the brain to stop the itch. The doctor had to persuade me to take it because I chose to come off all antidepressants some time ago, but it seems to be working. I only take one amitriptyline at night and it's just ten milligrams so it's a very low dose.

I don't have any answers yet. They still aren't sure of the cause and we don't know if it's psychological or neurological, but after quite some time, I've finally got some solutions and the situation is under control.

All sorts of things go wrong physically, and it's ongoing when you get to my age. It's up to us to stay on top of how we feel and to listen to what our bodies are telling us.

Another area which has been ignored and stigmatised is bladder weakness, something I've suffered with since I gave birth. I have to make sure I've been to the loo before I dance and if I do a purposeful appel in the Paso Doble (a step with a strong lowering of weight towards the floor), then I'll leak, no question.

So I was proud to be named as the face of the Always campaign Squeeze the Day in 2024, which started conversations all over the country about pelvic floor health, and I will talk about this till the cows come home if it helps the one in three women who experience bladder leaks to feel less alone.

When I was asked to front the campaign, my mother had many questions and was shocked that I'd agreed to do it. I guess that's a generational thing. There's still a long way to go but we are starting to talk more about the realities of female bodies.

'Oh, my God, you're not going to do *that*, are you?' said my mum. 'How could you?'

Well, somebody needs to do it and it might as well be me. There shouldn't be any shame about bladder leakage, or anything else that goes awry with the human body, it's no one's fault. And anything you detect in your body that you're concerned about or feels outside of the norm, don't be embarrassed to go to the doctor.

Mine once said to me, 'Your body's like a machine and when I look at you, that's what I see. My job is to give it an MOT and make sure it works.'

It's taken longer than I would have liked, but I finally feel that my hormones, wellbeing and all the issues associated with my female biology that have caused me so much anguish are, if not completely sorted, settled enough for me to live my life comfortably.

And beard-free.

I still get hairs on my chin, though. The first thing they do in the *Strictly* makeup chair is to pluck them all out and to be perfectly honest, it's the highlight of my week!

> 'Beautiful young people
> are accidents of nature,
> but beautiful old people
> are works of art.'
>
> ELEANOR ROOSEVELT

Each decade of my life has represented a different era for me. There have been losses, lessons and ups and downs in every one of them.

My twenties were dedicated to Corky and Mark and regrowth in the industry; my thirties were spent trapped in a marriage which was deeply unhappy.

I spent much of my forties finding myself again in between periods of misery, and hitting 50 was a shocker. That decade has probably been the hardest one of all, but it ended with the joy of *Strictly* and a rebirth which was as unexpected as it was beautiful.

My sixties have, so far, been characteristically turbulent but I'm hoping for some peace and calm. If I'm blessed with five more years, I'll be 70, which seems wild to me.

Always evolving and stepping into new versions of myself and managing shifts in perspectives and priorities.

Unfortunately, it also means getting older and the passage of time can be awfully cruel. My mother despises getting old. Hates it with a passion.

She looks at herself in the mirror and gets quite upset with what she sees, although I think she looks incredible. She's still going up ladders at 88 years of age and won't give in to sitting in a chair. She's always up and about cleaning, cooking, doing her dusting, making all the beds or putting fresh linen on.

She's also as sharp as a tack and keeps her brain active with little tricks like reciting the alphabet backwards and testing her memory by naming all the prime ministers of her lifetime in order. There was one time she got the list wrong and was so cross with herself that she sat down and wrote them out, starting all the way back in 1937 with Stanley Baldwin.

I'm not going to claim that the ageing process doesn't bother me because that would be a porkie pie, and if there was a pill to reverse or even slow down the advancing years then I'd neck the whole bottle.

Having the benefit of experience and knowledge you've gathered feels quite powerful and I do feel that getting to 60 was like reaching the top of a very steep mountain.

Only at that point did I start to come down the other side.

But I don't think getting old is something anyone particularly relishes. I don't like that it slows me down. I can't dance flat out any more or anything like as much as I want to, and my body no longer moves like a young whippersnapper and that frustrates me. I've also got an issue with my back which I have to watch, but I'll put my dance shoes on and I'll have a bloody good go.

None of us get a choice in the matter of ageing so we might as well do it gracefully, and we owe it to ourselves to look after our bodies and our minds as much as we can. I choose to take care of my weight and skin and am constantly making decisions based around them. I've sacrificed doughnuts, cookies and cakes because I know how harmful sugar is and I told you before that I avoid processed food like the plague.

I've accepted that my metabolism has ground to a shuddering halt, meaning I have to take control and watch how much and how often I eat. I tend to miss breakfast and try to stick to an 18-hour intermittent fasting schedule which allows me to eat within a six-hour window.

I have to be strict with myself, although most of my discipline and awareness around portion size and nutrition has been instilled throughout my life by my mother. She's always been trim and even today she is fastidious about what she eats and weighs herself daily.

She can't bear the feeling of extra pounds on her body and so makes it her mission to stay a good size for her build.

When I was growing up, we ate everything fresh – she worked her fingers to the bone but always made it a priority to give us our meat and two veg. Nothing out of a tin, ever. We didn't have cereals like cornflakes or Rice Krispies. By Friday it was egg and chips, but the potatoes were hand cut and the egg was our protein.

I do my best to hold back the years. I regularly practise yoga and meditation. I love to pray. I go to the Juice Master

Jason Vale's retreat in Portugal every year ahead of *Strictly* and thoroughly look forward to getting a good old cleanse. It clears my head and makes me feel like I can take on the world.

I got a Brass Monkey ice bath last year which has been a fantastic investment, and I try to have an invigorating two-minute dip every morning. It gives me a great dopamine hit. My mother thinks I'm crazy for doing it, but it works for me.

I also enjoy a sauna to ease the muscles and joints and very rarely drink these days, apart from the odd gin or a glass of red on special occasions. Even then I'm looking at the calorie count!

As regards to my skin, I haven't had that facelift, not yet! I'm not against cosmetic surgery – to each woman her own – but I use a NeoGen nitrogen plasma treatment which has tightened my jawline and reduced pigmentation. I started having these skin rejuvenation treatments back in February 2023 with Dr Johanna Ward at her clinic near London's Harley Street, and since then I've had roughly one a month. I particularly like it because it is totally non-invasive and the plume of super-heated nitrogen gas tricks your skin's natural defence mechanisms into creating lots of lovely collagen and elastin, the key elements for a youthful, radiant look. It isn't entirely pain-free but it is bearable and I noticed the positive effects after just three rounds of treatment.

Dr Ward also gives me a bit of Botox now and again, although I'm careful not to over-do that. Oh, and I try to make sure I drink plenty of water, too.

I'm pretty tough on myself if I eat something 'naughty' or miss my yoga session, but deep down I know I'm doing OK. I'm fit, healthy and in good shape and I think a lot of us forget to show ourselves kindness.

In an industry like dance, where there is so much criticism and people smile to your face but then annihilate you behind your back, the only person you can truly rely on to be kind is yourself.

I'm trying to remember that occasionally I need to pat myself on the back and recognise that. We all should.

Shirley's Shimmers

With the right support, menopause can be the
start of an exciting new chapter as a woman.
Embrace the transition to this next phase.

✘

Don't cling on to the past: adapt to change
and trust the process. Change often doesn't
make sense without the benefit of hindsight.

✘

Acknowledge feelings around change
and see it as an opportunity for growth.

✘

You can't stop time (if only …) but you can manage it by
staying active, eating well and listening to your body.

✘

While you may not have the get up and go you did in your
twenties, you've got years of experience and wisdom.
Your 21-year-old self couldn't handle what you can now.

✘

Ageing isn't a decline, it's a transformation.

✘

Move every day, breathe in fresh air and surround
yourself with people who love you.

✘

Life is a process of constantly learning but in order
to reap the rewards, we have to want to learn.

STEP SEVEN

Accept the Rise and Fall

SURVIVAL

'There we are,
once again.
Still breathing.'

AUDREY

*B*allroom dances can generally be categorised by the style of their movement. Take the Tango, for instance, which is danced low in the knees, with no rise and fall. It requires very articulate footwork, almost like how I've had to articulate my way through life.

The Waltz, by contrast, does feature a rise and fall action. A little, or should I say a lot, like my life.

Hats off to anyone who manages to 'waltz' through life avoiding any ups and downs – people who dodge the darker twists and turns must be a rare breed indeed.

For most of us, the journey is an unpredictable one with real-life rises and falls to steer through the whole time. I've experienced periods of joy when my world has been idyllic but I've also been down and out and had to fight with everything I had to keep going and keep believing while everything around me was falling apart.

The secret to survival, I think, is being able to embrace the sunshine and the storms, to appreciate life for both its beauty and ugliness and to understand that neither happiness nor hardship is ever permanent.

When you can dance in the rain, you're halfway there. I'm getting the hang of that.

I see my tough times as little pebbles which I gather up, put in a rucksack and carry on my back. Eventually the rucksack becomes too heavy and I can't go on. That's when I'll retreat to my bedroom, lock the door and take all that armoury off in private.

Hardly anyone sees that side of me because I can put my mask on anytime, anywhere. Whether I'm dolled up to the nines in a ballgown and a full face, or I'm makeup-free in a woolly sweater and my Marks & Spencer slippers, I have trained myself to be a certain way in front of other people.

It's that survival instinct kicking in, the defence mechanism which established itself in childhood, but it's also a form of denial and that's why it took me such a long time to admit to myself that I was struggling with my mental health.

It wasn't until my fifties when the menopause hit me like a ten-tonne truck and I really started digging into what was happening to me, that I realised my state of hopelessness was clinical depression.

As I explored the issue and talked to my mother about what my brother had battled with for much of his life until he died, it dawned on me that I'd suffered similar feelings intermittently since I was a young girl, but had never pinpointed a cause.

The difference between me and David, I suppose, was that I'd been able to cope a bit better with various situations. I had to appear strong, keep going, get to work, travel the world and raise a family. I never had the chance to sit down and reflect on what was going on inside my head because in my industry you keep moving until you pop your clogs.

I mentioned earlier that certainly during the early years of the menopause, there were times I felt myself heading down the same route as my brother. It's like plummeting into a black hole you can't climb up from. You're scratching away at the sides, trying and fighting to scramble your way up, but never quite managing before you fall back down again.

Mental health does not discriminate – prince or pauper, anyone can find themselves in that same desperate hole. And when nothing else is going right in your life either, clawing yourself out of that hole is even harder.

Compounding all of that is not having any sort of outlet to talk about how you're feeling. I'm an old-school suffering-in-silence type of person: don't communicate, don't speak up, don't let them see. Even when I was at my lowest ebb, people would ask how I was and I'd smile and say, 'I'm great, thanks.'

I didn't want anyone to think I was cracking up, so I kept up the façade, mechanically going through the motions of the day. These days I answer, 'Fair and partly cloudy,' which is closer to the truth.

Earlier in my life, I was dosed up on such a cocktail of pills and potions that my bathroom cabinet resembled a pharmacy – I was taking something to go to sleep and something else to wake me up, another pill for anxiety – but the problems weren't going away, they were still there waiting to be dealt with.

Not only were the meds failing to get to the root of my issues, they were also making me tired and sluggish, so a few years ago I made the decision to come off most of them.

I'm not anti-medication at all. If I'm jet lagged from travelling from the UK to the US and back again in the space of three days, I'll take half a sleeping tablet just to regulate my body clock. And if there are occasions when I need a little bit of extra help, I'll go ahead and ask for it.

Not so long ago I would never have admitted that publicly, thinking people would see me as weak. I've since done a complete 180 on it and now see it as a sign of great strength to be able to talk about these issues openly, but it's still not easy for me.

That stiff-upper-lip, keep-it-all-bottled-up restraint runs deep.

Whenever I have days where behind the eyes there's emptiness and all I want to do is come home, take a pill and go to bed, even now I struggle to share that with anyone. I just get through the day and hope that I wake up feeling brighter in the morning.

I always trust that the darkness will pass and things will get better because history shows this to be true. However, what I've found over 20 years in counselling is that you can talk about it until you're blue in the face but unless you're prepared to do something about it and unclip the baggage yourself, nothing will change.

I know I'll have anxiety until the end of my days. Panic attacks where my chest tightens, my heart starts racing, my body goes from cold to warm to raging hot and I'm sweating and uncomfortable and out of control.

But I have coping strategies in place now – I do meditation and I've got back into Bible reading which bookends my day in a positive way. As a committed Christian, my faith brings me enormous comfort. People who aren't religious at all don't need that, but I've found I do and it helps, so I always make time for the Lord and the little bond we've got going on.

Sometimes, if I'm tired or pushing it and giving it the whole 'I'm fine' routine, I'll sit down and have a cry with my mum and she'll listen.

Then she'll tell me to get a grip and sort myself out. Which I do.

> *'Mental illness is nothing to be ashamed of, but stigma and bias shame us all.'*
>
> BILL CLINTON

Losing David was catastrophic for our family. It's a pain that doesn't go away or even fade; you just get used to carrying it. Not so much a pebble in the rucksack as a boulder.

My lovely, kind, funny, caring, complicated big brother. He was only 44.

Why hadn't I made him my priority? My life had been racing along at the speed of light, far too fast to notice that his was on a collision course.

David, who was known as Kola to his mates, had fought to keep things steady. To me he was either the happiest soul in the world or he'd find himself stuck in these super-low moments and I often thought that he found it difficult to keep his life on track. My mother was his biggest support but that last year had been especially painful and Mum would regularly go and stay with him for months at a time to support him through the struggle.

His relationship with his partner and mother of his beloved daughter Mary had broken down, he had virtually stopped eating and we can see now that he was sinking.

David was always reluctant to seek professional help beyond the pills the doctor would prescribe – there was one occasion my mother drove him all the way to the hospital but he refused to get out of the car after spotting some old associates from the Leasowe and being overcome with shame, fearing they'd see him as weak.

It is agonising to know how close he came to getting the help that might have saved him. Just another 'what if' to add to a list which is already as long as my arm.

By December 2003 my mum had been living at David's for about eight weeks, helping him through this latest tough spot, and she was completely spent. I thought she needed a break so persuaded her to come down to London to watch Mark perform a solo in his school Christmas carol concert at St Paul's Church in Covent Garden.

'David will be fine,' I assured her. 'Come on, it'll do you good.'

I had no idea about the true extent of David's illness – had I any concept of how poorly he was, there is no way I'd have pushed my mum to travel and allowed him to be left alone. My understanding of mental health back then was tenuous at best. Mum had her reservations about leaving him, but David encouraged her to go too and so she agreed to come for one night.

After Mark's concert, I phoned David at home to check in on him, but got no reply, which suddenly gave me a horrible sense of foreboding. Worried, I phoned his ex, Eileen, and asked if she could pop round and see if he was OK, which she agreed to do. By now it was approaching midnight, so when she didn't call back, we went to bed assuming it must be all right.

I still remember the following morning as clear as day, walking down the stairs to find police officers standing at my front door. It was 6am and I'd let Mark stay out the night before, so my first thought was that something dreadful had happened to him.

'Mrs Rich?' asked the officers.

And I realised they were looking for my mother, not me. She was standing just behind me, having been woken by the doorbell.

I stepped aside.

'Mrs Rich, I'm so sorry to tell you that your son is dead.'

My poor mother let out a gasp of horror as her legs buckled and she fell to her knees. And right there, our whole world collapsed.

The next few hours passed by in a hazy blur of tears, confusion and utter disbelief. We needed to get back home as quickly as possible and it was Sammy who kindly drove Mum and I all the way there that Friday night. The traffic along the M6 was terrible and we hadn't been able to get hold of anybody at the mortuary, so we were blind about the living nightmare we were stepping into.

Eileen had found David after our phone call and the poor woman was in bits. I can't imagine the hell she went through that night. There was Mary to think of too, the beautiful daughter

David adored and who idolised him. She was only ten and while they might not have lived together at that time, he never let that girl down because he remembered what it was like for us as kids sitting by the window waiting in vain for our feckless father.

David broke that cycle by always coming for Mary exactly when he'd promised and taking such good care of her.

When you lose a loved one to suicide it leaves so many unanswered questions. It completely changed me. How could it not? I've been through every emotion in the years since. I was angry at the beginning. I was angry at everything, angry at the world, angry at myself.

Angry, angry, angry.

If only I'd taken some time to be more communicative with him, if only I'd stopped what I was doing and really noticed how much he was struggling.

I was so wrapped up in my own life – as well as Mark I had Derek and his sister Julianne to take care of, and my marriage to Corky was in tatters – that I wasn't alert as to how much trouble David was in. I didn't see the warning signs but I'm not sure I'd have known what to look for anyway.

There are a million and one things I wish I could change or have done differently and believe me, I've tortured myself over every one of them. But I knew that if I wanted to continue to be there for my son and help look after Mary, I had no choice but to find a way through.

And my way has been to channel my grief into helping other people.

My 50th birthday in the States was dedicated to a big suicide charity over there and I stipulated no gifts, just donations. We collected around $60,000.

I have also become involved with the charities Campaign Against Living Miserably (CALM) and Suicide & Co, and do a lot of public speaking around the subject – every speech I give is for David, people like him and for those who love them.

I would never wish any of this on another family, and I will never forget the hours I've sat with my mum while she's cried, wracked with guilt over the fact she left him to come and stay with me.

It doesn't matter how many people say so flippantly, 'Oh, don't blame yourself' – they don't know. Those final chats, those final hours, you play them over on repeat.

It's painful on a daily basis but I've stopped asking why he did it. Instead, I think about the fact that he must have done it because he was in a place so dark that none of us spotted it.

After David died, Mary came to live with me in London for a while before going to boarding school in Wales, where she thrived. She's in her early thirties now, has a gorgeous home where she's very happy with a great job as a healthcare scientist and a lovely partner called Augustine – Steen, my son calls him. It's a very special relationship; you can really feel the love when you're around them.

Mary has everything she needs and will never go short while I'm alive. We talk every week and she really is the most exceptional young woman – she suffers with Crohn's disease and there is always something going on with her health, but she gets on with things and doesn't let it hold her back. She's also the spitting image of her dad and has his big brown eyes and the same-shaped mouth.

If I'd known back then what I know now, I do think David would still be alive today. That makes me even more determined to keep talking about mental health and raising awareness around suicide prevention. I feel such a responsibility, given my platform and my experience, to bring this conversation out of the shadows and into the public consciousness.

Sunlight. Lots more sunlight.

Until we lost David, I didn't realise the numbers of people touched by suicide in some way. I hear of many tragic stories because the grief-stricken families left behind write to me, so it never feels too far away. I will keep fighting for them and for David.

I talk about him every day. I miss him every day.

All my material possessions became meaningless because I knew I would have traded absolutely everything I owned to have had one more moment with him.

We are but a fleeting glance. There aren't any pockets in a coffin; there's no luggage rack. In the end, you leave this world as you entered it: with nothing. Because you can't take any of it wherever you're going next.

I'd like to see if I can reach my brother through a medium one day. Is he floating? Is he resting? He's often around, I feel his presence and sometimes see what I think is his shadow.

Had he lived, I know he would have been right here by my side, my bodyguard, enjoying every moment of everything I ever did.

He was such a proud brother. And I'll always be proud to be his sister.

'Life is truly known only to those who suffer, lose, endure adversity and stumble from defeat to defeat.'

ANAÏS NIN

To me my mother is bulletproof and going to live forever. I tell her that every day: 'You're going to outlive us all.' So to be confronted with her mortality in 2018 was the cruellest of shocks and something I hadn't steeled myself for.

I was at the British championships in Blackpool and it was a Tuesday, the day of the amateur Latin, which is the biggest day in the dance calendar. My phone rang and I saw it was Mum calling.

'Hi,' I answered. 'I've only got a couple of minutes.'

'I just thought I'd better tell you something,' she said, almost matter-of-factly. The whole conversation was Audrey to a T.

'Oh, right, what's that?'

'I've got cancer.'

I fell to my knees. I couldn't even speak. I broke into a thousand pieces.

I left the festival and went straight to Wallasey where she was living, just outside the Leasowe estate. I found her cool as a cucumber and taking everything in her stride.

You'd never have known she'd just received such terrible news.

She coped far better than I ever did. I didn't cope at all, truth be told. I tried to be good in front of her and hold it together, but I was a mess because I couldn't bear to think of losing her.

The cancer was in the colon and she'd been experiencing unwellness for a little while – one doctor I'd taken her to see in the US had her jumping up and down to check for appendicitis and I remember we'd had a good laugh about that at the time.

Little did we know.

It was when we came back to the UK and she visited her GP here that they ran some tests and found a lump that was cancerous. They took her in and removed the lump and this was one of the toughest times I've ever faced, seeing my strong, independent mother in hospital.

Once she had recovered from the operation, she went back to see the consultant, who informed her that there were still some lymph nodes remaining. Without chemotherapy, there was a risk the cancer would spread to other parts of her body. She was strongly advised to take the treatment but my mother was adamant that she didn't want it.

She said to the doctor, 'Would you give it to your grandmother?'

'Off the record?' he asked.

'Absolutely,' said my mum.

'OK, no I wouldn't.'

'Well then I don't want it.'

'There's a risk …'

'I'm willing to take that chance,' she said.

End of discussion.

She turned the chemo down and of course I was terrified for her, but I also believe it would have killed her. She was 81 and just a slip of a thing and I don't think she would have survived the gruelling rounds of treatment cycles.

I nursed her through that summer and beyond, doing the cleaning, washing and cooking – which was disastrous because I'm hopeless at all things culinary. I administered her injections and she was so gracious about everything, even telling me I was a great cook, which I knew was a fib.

My mother is proof that miracles happen, because five years on, she's alive and kicking and in remission. She goes once a year to get checked, but she's still up and about, cleaning her ornaments and doing her own washing and ironing again.

She has a television in her bedroom, there's one in my room and another downstairs and she has all three turned on at 100 decibels so when she's moving around – because she never sits still – she doesn't miss a minute of the programme she's watching. Ha!

I've tried to talk to her about her smoking but she says it's one of her luxuries in life whenever I bring it up. She's smoked off and on all her life – she actually gave up for several years after my brother died, but later went back to it – and there's no telling her. Not even the fact she has chronic obstructive pulmonary disease (COPD), which can make her breathing difficult, will make her quit. I've been there when she's practically choked to death, then she'll stop coughing and say, 'I'm all right now, let me go and get a fag.'

She's the most extraordinary human being I've ever met in my life. Indestructible.

And the way she faced up to her cancer and got the better of it without wallowing or whining reinforced all she's ever taught me about resilience and pressing on.

'You may not realise it when it happens, but a kick in the pants may be the best thing in the world for you.'

WALT DISNEY

Almost immediately after starting on *Strictly*, I had a rude awakening that being in the public eye went hand in hand with a fair amount of unwanted attention. Among the weird (and also wonderful) messages which were flooding my social media accounts, was one from a man called Kyle Shaw who was claiming to be the biological son of my late brother.

I think we initially assumed it was a crank – my manager at the time was dealing with anything like that and said she would handle it – so none of us gave it too much thought. We had no idea that this was the start of a seven-year stalking campaign of terror which would leave me living in fear for my life.

The messages from Shaw escalated quickly, becoming very graphic, and he was soon hounding me through every channel possible. Via Facebook Messenger, Twitter and Instagram, he was demanding a DNA test and accusing me of killing David.

'Just a reminder, my dad is dead because of you, because you left him alone. He's dead. You killed him. You murdered him. You did this. Why did you leave my dad to die?'

That's one of the milder, more printable messages.

We called the police and he was warned not to contact me again. That warning did nothing. Not only did he continue to harass and attack me, but he also started bombarding other members of my family, including my elderly mother. He'd seek out my friends and post the most awful messages to them, using language I can't even bring myself to repeat.

I had to increase my security with CCTV and have an extra alarm system put in at my house. I became increasingly nervous going out anywhere and I stopped using public transport altogether. He'd told me to look over my shoulder and that he'd always be there.

He posted a photograph of my house and car on social media with a message that read, 'You ruined my life, I'll ruin yours and everyone's around you.'

When my debut novel came out in 2023, he sent me a deluge of messages threatening to turn up at one of the dates on the promotional tour.

'I'll be there, Shirley. I'll be at the show. I'll be everywhere, lurking in the wings.'

What should have been a happy time in my life celebrating writing a book I was proud of, turned into an enormously distressing experience. I was always on high alert, in permanent fight-or-flight mode because he'd made it abundantly clear how much he despised me, despite us never having met.

I'd never even heard of the boy before he first contacted me in 2017.

At one point he somehow got hold of my then-partner Danny's phone number and called him, saying he knew where we both lived and describing my recent movements.

Everywhere I went I'd be scanning the area, thinking, is that him? Is he over there? To live in a state of hypervigilance like that is horrendous and emotionally draining. It's the only thing you think about 24 hours a day and when you're trying to focus on something else, you can't get it off your mind.

I'd block him but he'd just set up new profiles, sometimes even in my brother's name, and I was receiving daily messages telling me how much he hated me and that he wished it was me who was dead.

He even went to the extreme of following my mother around the supermarket in Liscard and confronted her, which was a horrifying experience for a woman in her eighties. That was the final straw for me. I moved her from Wallasey down to London and in with me where I could look after her and she's been here ever since.

I didn't feel safe in my own home and had sleepless nights worrying about what he was going to do. Would he put a bomb through the letterbox? Or try to set the house on fire? I had smoke detectors installed everywhere. He'd shown he was prepared to follow a little old lady round the supermarket, what else was he capable of doing to frighten the living daylights out of my family?

I had to completely change the way I lived my life. The BBC gave me additional security in and around the studio when we were filming and on the *Strictly* tour, I was picked up and dropped off at every venue door to door. The measures they put in place were reassuring – they did everything to make me feel comfortable, but I was on edge all the time.

Throughout this ordeal I was in constant touch with the police, especially when he made threats, as he often did, to kill himself. I was just as terrified he'd harm himself as I was he would me.

Contact would usually start around the beginning of August, when the publicity for *Strictly* kicked off, and from there the harassment would build and continue right the way through the series and into the New Year. I could always tell if he was high or on something, because the messages would intensify.

Towards the end of February, it would tail off and he tended to go a bit quiet, but then the cycle would begin again the following August. It felt neverending.

Merseyside Police were helpful but the system makes it very difficult for charges to be brought, which leaves victims trapped. It's as if you have to come to physical harm before the law steps in to protect you. All I could do was gather the correspondence and keep passing it on to the police. Eventually, in December 2023, more than six years after the first message, Shaw was arrested and later charged with stalking. Police had seized his computer and phones, but at the early court hearings, he pleaded not guilty. It looked like the case was headed for trial where I would have to give evidence.

The thought of that caused me huge anxiety. My mother would also have had to take the stand, as well as friends and family who were witnesses.

Thankfully, in February 2025, he changed his plea to guilty – the overwhelming evidence had him bang to rights so I'm not sure he really had any other option. And on 1 April 2025, the judge at Liverpool Crown Court handed down a 20-month suspended sentence. He was also banned from contacting me, my mother, Danny or my niece Mary ever again.

I was satisfied that justice had been done – I had no interest in seeing the boy go to jail. He's a very troubled person who needs help, not prison. The psychiatric report revealed a damaged person whose life had been blighted by mental illness, homelessness and drug abuse. I just hope he continues to get the support he needs to rehabilitate.

I didn't go to court to see him sentenced but I did provide a victim impact statement, which was read out. Here is an extract of what I wrote:

> Over the years, the behaviour has had a dramatic impact on not only my life but on that of those dearest to me, including my mother, my niece, my friends and those close to me. He has accused both my mother and I of killing my brother, which was extremely painful and distressing. My brother was loved dearly by us all and to this day is missed.
>
> I have made it clear that I do not want any contact with him or any member of his family. I feel I am constantly looking over my shoulder and I am worried

when in public that he may turn up and cause me personal harm or hurt those I love the most.

I just want him to stop and get on with his life so that me and my family can get on with ours.

I wanted him to know how he had made us feel for all these years. He's taken my peace of mind away from me and I don't think I'll ever fully recover it. I will never feel completely safe again.

But I'm relieved it's over and we can all move on. The weight has been lifted and yet again, I'm battered, bruised but still standing.

That in-built pluckiness to keep marching on, no matter what, had come through for me once more.

'The darkest nights produce
the brightest stars.'

ANONYMOUS

When my dad died in April 2021, I felt very little. I was waiting to feel *something*, to have any sort of reaction to his passing despite everything that had gone before, but none came.

I went to his funeral where I felt certain people were looking at me … there were definite disdainful stares in my direction, probably because it was shortly after my autobiography had been released where I'd described him as a 'deadbeat dad'.

Part of me is sorry I ever put that line in the book because I know it looked terribly stark in print, but I'm always honest and that was my truthful experience of him as a father.

I always made the effort with him. Every time I came back home to the Wirral, I'd go and see him. But it was never reciprocated and we had many fallouts over the years.

I once wrote him a five-page letter pouring my heart out after he'd been awful about David. I told him that David had been more of a dad to his daughter Mary than he'd ever been to us. My father could be vindictive, too. When his other son, Mark, from a later relationship died suddenly in 2018, he told me I wasn't welcome at the funeral, which really upset me. I'd been quite close to Mark, who was my half-brother after all, but my dad said I wasn't to attend and he shouted this down the phone to me.

'Don't you be turning up at the funeral. You won't be wanted there!'

Months later, my mother bumped into him by chance while she was out for a drink with my auntie Mavis, and from what I've been told, they had it out over that. This little five-foot woman went for my dad's jugular and really let him have it.

Astonishingly, though, Mum never once slagged him off the whole time I was growing up, which I think was very honourable. She'd have been well within her rights to tear him to shreds because of the way he'd treated the three of us, leaving us all in the lurch and then continually letting us down.

'You'll draw your own conclusions,' is all she'd say.

I thought he might have stepped up after my brother died and been more present for Mary, his granddaughter who had lost her father in those most tragic of circumstances.

But he couldn't have cared less.

It is what it is.

I do remember the press doorstepped him when I got the *Strictly* job and he told them where to get off. 'If you need any comments on that girl's career,' he said, 'take it up with her mother. She's the one who raised her.'

Interesting, isn't it? He did have some decency about him and I think to other people he was probably quite a fun man. He was a good-looking fella and I've heard he was sociable to sit with over a drink, but that doesn't change how he treated me and I know he was a difficult person throughout his life.

I had a brief 'moment' at his funeral when they brought his coffin in, but it was only a slight wobble which passed as quickly as it began and didn't become anything more than that.

His wife died shortly after him and my auntie Barbara, his sister, phoned me.

'You're entitled to something of your dad,' she said.

'He gave me nothing when he was alive, and I'll take nothing now he's dead,' I replied. 'Give it to somebody else, I don't want it.'

The only thing I asked for was a photograph of him because I'd have rather liked to have one. But they wouldn't give me one, so there you go.

I do sometimes worry about myself with regard to feelings. I tend to put my troubles into a Pandora's box – I've got a garage full of them – and I leave them there. Thankfully, I'm able to compartmentalise very easily; I would get overwhelmed if everything was mushed together. If a box is ever opened, I deal with whatever it is there and then before closing it again.

But even when people die who have been close to me, I find myself suppressing the tears. I want to sob my heart out because I know it's good for the soul but it's as if I have to block it. I spent so many years having to be strong for David and then for my mum, that I got used to stifling. If I feel a wave of something coming, I get out my imaginary hammer and nail and batter it back down.

'Not today, sunshine.'

Occasionally I don't quite manage to do that – one time I lost it on the *This Morning* sofa when I was doing an interview about David and then the photos of me 'breaking down' were plastered all over the media, which was the last thing I wanted.

For me, it's best to be as hard as a hobnail boot and wear grief and sadness alone.

And keep the faith, privately, that the sun will shine again.

Shirley's Shimmers ✦

Learn to let go of what you can't control;
this will free up energy to invest in what you can.

✕

Accept that the struggle can be part of your growth.

✕

If you can roll with the punches,
you'll recover quicker from those blows.

✕

Don't be afraid to ask for help if
you're finding life challenging.

✕

It's OK not to be OK – acknowledge
your feelings without judgement.

✕

Find an outlet for grief, somewhere
positive you can channel it.

✕

Strength isn't defined by how often you're
tested but by how you keep going.

STEP EIGHT

Gain Alignment

BALANCE

'There should be
no regrets in life,
only lessons.'

AUDREY

*W*hen we talk about the alignment of the body in dance, we're referring to the positioning of the head, spine, shoulders and hips. It's about maintaining a beautiful straight line from top to toe, with the weight evenly distributed and the core engaged.

Great alignment is the holy grail; the foundation for good balance. The dancer can use that centre of gravity to perform with greater control and stability and, as a teacher, when I see it happen, it's like everything else clicks into place.

Transferring that into the everyday, however, is a Cha-Cha-Challenge and a half. If you were to ask me how to strike a healthy balance between work, rest and play, I could give you some excellent advice. I'd tell you all about the importance of setting clear boundaries, good time management and making sure to practise self-care.

I'd talk to you about why it's so important that we find peace in this busy, noisy, relentless world and spend meaningful time with the people who make us happy.

But although I'd be able to tell you all the things I think *you* should do, it wouldn't mean I'm doing any of them myself. I can talk a good game all right, but the truth is I'm married to my work. That's probably why I don't have a lover!

I've still to learn how to relax properly – the thought of having a lie-in, vegetating in my own bed, is completely alien to me – and I find it virtually impossible to switch off. It's a definite flaw in my character and there have been periods, especially when I was teaching full-time, when I came close to burnout. There were days when I didn't know how the hell I was going to muster the energy to carry on with the three major dance competitions a year, private lessons all year round, and jetting across the world to teach, demonstrate and judge. I've globetrotted my whole career but never had the chance to explore any of the places I've visited.

Fly in, do the job, fly out, move on to the next task.

My work is never routine, it's always varied. Just when I think I've got a week off, ten other jobs come hurtling in and although it means my schedule is as punishing as ever, I like the excitement of that. It keeps this life interesting, not ever really knowing what's around the corner. And when it's something I know I'll enjoy or is focused on an area close to my heart, I don't like to turn it down.

My PA Harry makes me laugh because he's always saying I need to take a rest. My mother, too.

'OK, no problem,' I say. 'You find some space in the diary and I'll do it.'

Meetings, interviews, teaching – the only bit of down time I get is in the car and that's often spent talking to my gay gaggle Alan and Nathan.

Those around me say, 'Shirley you need to chill.'

A doctor told me that too. 'If you don't slow down, you'll be in a wooden box in five years.'

But I think that if I did slow down, that's what would kill me.

There's no chance to pause for breath because from the start of the year to the very end, my calendar never lets up. In January I have the *Strictly* tour and they allow me one day off from that to go and judge at the United Kingdom Open to the World championships in Bournemouth. Then in March it's the NYDF championship over in New York and I teach all the couples in the week leading up to that. Once I'm back in the UK, it's the run-up to Blackpool and the British Open to the Worlds in May.

After that, there are dance camps throughout the summer, the *Strictly* launch in September which runs through to Christmas, the International championships at the Royal Albert Hall in October, plus all my own private lessons, press commitments and other TV work in between my charity work and visiting my grandson.

I often promise my mother a few days off together and she'll nod knowingly, 'Well, we'll see about that, won't we?'

Since joining *Strictly* in 2017 my work has become much more wide-ranging, but the load hasn't lightened and my refusal to take a day off is something I'm known for in the industry.

'She never stops working,' some say. And I know one or two people make fun of me behind my back and think I'm mercenary, driven purely by money, but for three reasons they're completely wrong.

Firstly, my work is my cocoon, my cushion. Every day I start early and finish late, staying on that treadmill to avoid dealing with the more emotional matters I don't care to think about.

Secondly, I have a scarcity mindset stemming from my child-hood and the days when we were permanently skint. It's a pattern of thinking I can't help: what if there's no job next week? What if all this disintegrates? Who knows what's around the corner?

And finally – most importantly – I *love* what I do. Dance makes me whole. It's freedom and expression and it's what I enjoy doing most in the world.

Every day is a new day for me: new people, new lessons, new adventures, new results. I want to talk about it all the time to the point where those around me practically beg me to change the subject!

It's more than an obsession; it's a way of life.

But I'm also aware that I need to learn how to take it down a few notches and experience some stillness. My mother is the queen of that. She has her morning routine where she has her breakfast and potters about, then every afternoon she goes upstairs for a rest on the bed where she'll watch old episodes of *Coronation Street*. I know I should take a leaf out of her book.

I am trying. From now on, I want to make sure that any place I'm visiting for work, whether that's Dubai, China or even just the Isle of Man, there are a few days either side of competitions to take in the sights.

Also, and hear me out on this one, while *Strictly* has added to my work commitments, it has also given me a much-needed escape route which has helped me realign. There are so many people in dance who feel it's their way or the highway. They don't see their flaws or their mistakes and it's exasperating and exhausting. It's still a man's world and although women are trying and fighting to be seen and heard, we've got an awful long way to go before we're treated as equals. The men don't like the fact we're trying to move and change with the times.

Doing *Strictly* at the end of the year, followed by the nationwide tour, gives me a little break from the ongoing dance-industry dramas, bickering and in-fighting. I get to extricate myself from all the blithering for a while and that has been beneficial to me.

I'm also getting better at handling stress with age. When a high-pressure situation arises, I calm my heartbeat down with steady breathing and feel safety in the knowledge that this is only temporary. Take a step back, don't panic, and this too shall pass.

That's a good one to remember and the older you get the more you realise how true it is.

'Never get so busy making a living that you forget to make a life.'

DOLLY PARTON

If I have very little balance now, I had even less when Mark was growing up and my biggest regret in life is not being around as much as I would have liked. I wasn't there when he had chicken pox or when my brother decided it would be a good idea to chop off all his gorgeous curls. I lost count of the number of first days of term I was absent for.

I missed five Christmases because Corky and I were in Japan.

I remember one terrible time I took Mark to the dentist who said he had too many teeth in his mouth and needed four extractions.

'So, we'll take two out today and make another appointment for the others,' said the dentist.

'No,' I replied, 'take them all out today.'

I said that under a lot of pressure because I was so busy and worried that I wouldn't have time to come back. As his mother, I wanted to be with my son for the procedure, to hold his hand and comfort him, but I couldn't guarantee I'd be able to make a second appointment. What a mistake. Although I was there with him the whole time, Mark was there sobbing with the pain and I shouldn't have put him through it. Even now, nearly 30 years later I still feel full of remorse over that. It hurts my heart just thinking about it.

Corky and I were flying all over the States to teach and demonstrate as well as taking trips to far-flung places and that meant long spells away from our son. He was safe and looked after by my mother, who had moved over to America to help out with the childcare, but I've carried the guilt my whole life.

Until I retired from competing in 1996, bowing out in a blaze of glory with those historic back-to-back British Open to the World titles with Corky when Mark was ten, it was my mother who raised him. I often notice he's got the same traits she passed on to me – he's robust and a hard worker, a researcher of his trade and gives his all to anything he puts his mind to. He is so focused in all he does.

Just the other day he said that in order to enjoy a holiday, he has to feel like he's earned it. That's my mother through and though.

She did a fantastic job with him and I'm so thankful to her for giving up her own life to step in and scoop us up. But that doesn't change the fact that children need their parents, which simply wasn't something I paid much heed to as a 25-year-old new mother.

Now I look at my grandson Banksi with his dad together and I do think, 'Wow, I never experienced any of this ...' Through Mark and his incredible skills as a father, I'm witnessing what could have been, should have been, but never was.

It's beautiful to see Mark being the kind of daddy who gives his son the gift of time and doing all the fatherly things I wish I'd had with my dad. But although I'm full of admiration for him, it's tinged with sadness.

I look back at so many things I should have done differently as a mother, but what do you know when you're young and trying to make a career in an industry which is tough as hell?

Dancing is all I've ever known, all I've ever done.

Mark and I have spoken about this and he doesn't hold it against me at all. He's always been wise beyond his years and takes a philosophical perspective on the situation, insisting that me and his dad did what we had to do. Because we worked so hard, we all lived in a nice home and Mark got to enjoy many experiences I could only have dreamed of as a little girl.

One way I console myself is by remembering that because my mum gave up work to look after him full-time, he had her complete and undivided attention. Their time together was never on a deadline and because of one bad experience with a childminder I never left him with anyone else but my mother.

And you know what? He's turned out to be a wonderful man, so maybe between us all, we did OK. He is such a caring guy and he's found a real winner in BC, who is an all-round good person and such a calming presence. I love the fact that she lives in the moment and is a de-fueller of all fires. I'm trying to take inspiration from her when it comes to being more Zen and finding that elusive balance, because she comes from a different universe to me.

She has her priorities right and nothing ever appears to get to her. She's never in a fluster or stress and I'm learning a lot from her.

And here's a tip I got from my mother: never cross the daughter-in-law. Don't ever get in between their fights and do not, under any circumstances, voice an opinion unless you are explicitly asked for one, otherwise you won't have the relationship you want with your son. Understand and respect those boundaries even if it's occasionally hard to swallow and you shouldn't go far wrong.

It's difficult not to wonder how my life might have turned out differently with a bit more alignment. If Sammy and I had more personal time together and hadn't been so influenced by other people such as Bob Dale and our teacher Nina Hunt, maybe we could have created a better marriage. We could have taken holidays and had more me-and-him time.

It was the same with Corky. We were so focused on getting his dancing career off the ground, then having Mark and travelling all over the world, that we had very little time for each other. Our relationship was an afterthought.

Relationships with family and partners should always come first, a lesson I learned a little too late. Be present and prioritise the people who matter while you still can.

> *'The key to successful work-life balance is to not be afraid to fail at it. You will drop the ball on something; the trick is knowing which balls are made of rubber and which are made of glass.'*
>
> NORA ROBERTS

My good friend Terrie once said to me, 'When I die, Shirley, I'm going to slide into my coffin sideways shouting, "I had a ball!" When you die, you're going in screaming, "I worked myself to death!"'

Sounds about right.

In 2024 I thought I'd done exactly that when a routine mammogram identified some abnormalities in my breast tissue. The daftest thing of all was, I'd been so busy with work that I'd planned to reschedule the appointment until Amy Dowden MBE, my wonderful student, friend and *Strictly* colleague warned me not to put it off. You will probably know that she was diagnosed with stage three breast cancer in 2023 at the age of just 32, and when someone who has been through everything that girl has looks you in the eye and tells you to do something, you damned well listen.

I knew she was right.

I changed my work schedule and went along for the screening at a mobile NHS unit stationed in a Sainsbury's car park and three days later I received a gut-wrenching phone call. I was to go to King's College hospital for further investigation.

I was beside myself – there's a history of cancer in the family and my mother had not long recovered from her own battle. She was in remission, but the trauma was still very raw.

The doctor at King's, thankfully, cut to the chase. I'm not a fan of waffle at the best of times and this was definitely not an occasion to beat around the bush.

'I don't want to alarm you,' he said (too late for that), 'but we found something we're not too sure about and we'll need to do a 3D mammogram to get a closer look at it.'

This was a scan using a more advanced machine which allows radiologists to examine breast tissue intricately, layer by layer, but even that didn't provide any further clarification.

I therefore needed a biopsy and it was then that I fell apart. When you start hearing words like 'biopsy', which feel so loaded, it triggers your worst fears. I begged them to perform it that same day, knowing I wouldn't have been able to stand any delay.

Doctors did three biopsies in the end under local anaesthetic and then I went home, all bandaged up and facing a torturous wait for the results.

That week was a living hell. I was a complete nervous wreck and there were a lot of tears as I prepared myself for the news. I was convinced that a lifetime of working myself silly had caused this. All this refusing to take my foot off the gas was now going to kill me.

I'd done this to myself.

I tried to keep myself occupied while I waited. I'd been open about the situation on social media and I also did a sit-down interview with the *Sun* – as I said before, it's always been important to me to share the highs and the lows of my life with the public.

But more than that, I wanted to speak directly to other women and urge them not to delay their mammograms – nothing is more important than your health and early detection is key.

Eight days after the biopsy – the longest eight days of my life – the hospital phoned with my results. I don't have the words to describe the sheer relief when I was told I had the all-clear with no sign of cancer present. I felt the pent-up anxiety instantly dissolve and was then overcome with emotion.

This had been a wake-up call and I vowed to learn from it. I'd been lucky this time but if ever there was a sign to slow down and find a different pace, this was it. I was going to do things a lot differently.

Famous last words.

I'd love to be able to tell you that I was jolted into taking regular breaks and carving out 'me time' for meditation and healing, but I'm still searching for that pause button. I know it's somewhere. Maybe I don't want to find it.

As I said earlier, I'm hopeless when it comes to taking my own advice.

'Almost everything will work again if you unplug it for a few minutes, including you.'

ANNE LAMOTT

Sometimes I wish I could chuck my smartphone into the ocean and watch it sink. These blasted things rob us of so much time. They're a pollution, a total nightmare and they're doing more harm than good.

When I go to the airport, everyone is on their iPads or phones. There are people at tables in restaurants brainlessly scrolling. Nobody sits around having a natter any more and it often feels like you're trapped in the land of the doomed.

What's become of us? Social media is killing off interaction between family, friends. These young girls who don't think they're pretty enough because they see everyone else through a filter, not realising that they're comparing themselves to something which doesn't exist. Off they go to get their Botox, boob jobs and bum lifts when they're barely out of their teens.

If you're on your phone doom-scrolling all day long, you're not socialising, you're not out there communicating, networking. I've never seen anything else with such a hold over people – I watch dancers finish their lessons and the first thing they do is check their phone.

What's that doing for you? What are you learning? Why are we so interested in what other people are doing? Other people whose sole aim is to make it appear as if they have the perfect life when they're probably as miserable as sin.

It's all smoke and mirrors.

The effect this is having on our collective mental health, especially among the young, is frightening. Research shows a direct link between smartphone usage and increased anxiety, depression, self-esteem struggles and insomnia in our teenagers.

That's apart from the dangers of people pretending to be someone they're not, money scammers, kids accessing porn, suicide and self-harm content.

It's also worrying how much these devices know about us. I was talking recently about getting a mug designed for Dance With Us and the next time I opened up my phone, a stream of targeted adverts for mugs came up. They're listening to us and it's hard not to get paranoid about that.

And yet, I'm just as susceptible to the lure of the phone as the next person and managing my use of it is something I'm trying to get on top of. I absolutely recognise its hold over me, but breaking free of it is easier said than done and, frankly, I'm horrified by my own screen time stats.

Harry takes care of my social media posts now, but I will often scroll through my feed when what I should be doing is putting the thing down and picking up a book instead.

I know it makes me less productive and fills my brain with guff, giving me information overload with its 24/7 ding-ding-dinging. I keep it on and nearby round the clock because I have people in different time zones who need to be in touch with me.

I can't bring myself to turn it off.

Some clever people have no problem switching the phone off and shutting it away for the day. I admire that so much and plan on using my phone more mindfully and in moderation. There are strategies to help, such as using the 'Do Not Disturb' function for periods to stop the distractions and setting time limits on the use of certain energy-sapping apps.

I want to read more and write in my journal rather than being a slave to the screen. I want to prioritise my mental and physical wellbeing and make time to practise gratitude, not just to myself but to others – I like to send people handwritten cards of appreciation.

But I know only I can do this. My time and my focus are in my hands and if I want to reclaim it from the menace of the mobile, that is totally down to me.

'The bad news is time flies.
The good news is you're the pilot.'

MICHAEL ALTSHULER

A lot of people thought I might start to take it a little easier when I became a grandmother. It's true that Banksi has given me a new outlook on life and the joy of being his nanny is indescribable.

He was born in November 2023 and I want to spend as much time as I can with him. He's already got a quirky sense of humour. He loves music and likes to play the piano. He's very good at amusing himself – Mark was the same – and I think that says something about his character already.

I'm lucky to have a son who calls me every day, so I get all the updates as they're happening and I see Banksi all the time on FaceTime. That means despite the distance, I'm a very familiar figure to him, and it gives me the fuzziest of fuzzy feelings when I walk into their house and his adorable chubby arms stretch out for a cuddle.

I love getting him ready for bed into his jammies. He started to walk before he was one so perhaps that's an indication we have a mini dancer in the making. Time will tell.

I find myself thinking about him all the time, I only wish I got to see him a bit more. I don't want to miss out when he goes to school or when he's cast as an elf at the Christmas concert. I suppose the ideal scenario would be to split my time between here in the UK and the US where my family are.

BC told me recently, 'Shirley, you live the furthest away, but you make such a big effort to be here with us.' She probably didn't realise how much hearing her say that meant to me, but it was the most beautiful compliment she could have given me.

But although many assumed that I would start winding down a bit after he was born, it hasn't happened yet. I'm still at the top of my industry, doing the three big dance events a year and teaching whenever I can. I love the social outlet dancing provides and mixing in and around young people keeps my mind active.

I do feel torn, having missed out on so much of the beginning of Mark's life, and part of me is scared that I'm allowing my second shot to slip away. But I've got my mum who's in remission from cancer and has done so much for me over the decades that I owe her my undivided loyalty. Then I have the responsibility to all my dance couples and my commitments to *Strictly*, so I often feel I'm being pulled in different directions.

The most I'll do is slow down a touch. I'll never retire.

Carry on doing what you love while you're here because, let's face it, you're a long time dead.

Shirley's Shimmers

Cherish the relationships which nourish you.

✕

Time with loved ones is invaluable
and irreplaceable – ringfence it.

✕

Slowing down isn't giving up or being lazy.
It's a way of recharging your mind and body.

✕

A truly fulfilling life is about more than achievements
on a CV – it's about relationships and people.

✕

Switch your phone off for a while –
we all need to stop being such slaves to the tech.

✕

Pay attention to your energy levels
and do more of what fuels you.

STEP NINE

Trust Your Partner

CONNECTION

'Treat others as you'd
wish to be treated
yourself. If you can.'

AUDREY

*T*he dream for every dancer is finding a partner whose body speaks exactly the same language as your own. Someone you're in complete tune with, where every step together feels instinctive and effortless.

Professional dance partners have to depend on each other for physical and emotional support, developing an almost telepathic understanding where they never have to second guess. It's a connection like no other and you are so much more than just a team. It's a fusion of two people who continue moving forward together even when the going gets tough.

All of these qualities and traits mirror those of my closest relationships outside of dance.

I keep my circle of trust small and choose my friends with the same care and precision as the footwork in a perfectly executed Foxtrot.

I'm able to suss people out quite quickly and have developed a good intuition for a wrong'un over the years. I've met plenty of them! It means my red flag radar is strong and I can sniff out bad energy, although I do still occasionally misjudge it and end up getting hurt.

Hence the small circle.

I can count my ride-or-dies on the fingers of one hand; it's an inner sanctum that has been whittled down over the years to protect myself. The fewer people I let in, the less chance there is of being deceived, betrayed or sold down the river.

Of course, I have a wider network of people I know I can depend on and they know who they are. They'd be there in a heartbeat if I ever needed them.

But actually being able to trust people with my whole heart, to cry on their shoulder and show them the real, raw and unseen Shirley Ballas? It's just my mother and Mark.

I know when I tell them anything, it's not going any further. They are my partners in crime and the only people I trust 100 per cent.

They both serve very different purposes for me and I'd be lost without either one of them.

My mother for her straight-talking approach to life, her ability to cut through the bullshit, kick my butt into gear and shake me out of a funk.

Mark for his warmth and his intelligent framing of situations so that even if it's not what you want to hear, the message is delivered with empathy. He always sees things from both sides and manages to find a way to say, 'I get your point of view, but this is my perspective ...'

Everything he does is heartfelt. When he was playing the lead in *Jersey Boys* on Broadway and I went to see him for about the 27th time, the doorman said to me, 'We have actors here who walk straight past you, but not your Mark. He knows everybody's name. Forget his talent, his human relations are absolutely outstanding.'

As a mother, that was the greatest accolade I could have wished to hear.

When I first met my daughter-in-law, BC, she also quickly became part of my circle of trust. I kept on calling her CB by mistake and after a few times, she replied, 'OK, Shirbey!'

I immediately thought, 'Oh, I love this girl.'

She had the quick wit and sense of humour to give it to me back and I like that kind of banter. It's actually very Liverpool.

Other than those three, it's hard to imagine allowing anyone new in now and I keep everyone else at arm's length, only letting them inch closer if it's on my terms. Until someone has proved themselves to me over an extended period of time, I treat every-one with a large dollop of cynicism. I say that with some sorrow but unfortunately it's a defence mechanism built into my psyche as a result of past betrayals and disappointments.

Is it sensible or sad, my being so wary? I think it's sensible but I'll let you decide. I just know from experience that you've got to go through life keeping your wits about you and the only person you can completely depend on is yourself.

Especially since the breakup with Danny, I tend to approach everything and everyone without too many expectations and then if they let me down, it doesn't hurt as much.

And if they don't, I can be pleasantly surprised.

You can't replace time and I've already wasted too much of that on people I should never have given more than a second's thought to.

'A real friend is one who walks in when the rest of the world walks out.'

WALTER WINCHELL

You can barely move in a ballroom for all the egos.

Dance is such a fickle industry, full of piranhas who would sell their own grandmother if it meant they jumped one space higher up the rankings, and who make it their life's business to throw gasoline on everything.

When you go to an event or competition, on the surface it's all sparkles and sequins, but behind the scenes it can sometimes feel like a seething viper's nest. In this business, I quickly learned that I couldn't trust everyone. Some are in permanent competition mode; they're like trained assassins and the only thing on their mind is winning and being the star. Everybody wants something, walking around like they've got a bloody badge pinned to their shoulder.

I'm a people watcher, always have been, so I see them slithering around looking for ways to get themselves ahead, smiling to your face then speaking behind your back, harbouring a bitterness towards you. I still feel some are clutching on to the fact that, decades ago, I beat them to a title.

The moment somebody slags off someone else to me, I've got the measure of them, because if they can do that to one person, you can bet your bottom dollar they can do that to me. I know I'll be next the minute my back is turned.

Back in the early eighties when Sammy and I had that meteoric rise to the top of the tree, we were trouncing everybody. Boom, boom, boom. We didn't wait for dead men's shoes; we flew up the rankings and won everything in sight.

I went from that to Corky, a man who didn't know much about the industry, and suddenly I had to do the hard slog all the way back up. It was slow progress, sometimes ten paces backwards to move just one forward and I knew everyone was laughing at us. But we persevered even though we hardly had an ounce of respect from an industry which saw us as mere beginners.

And even when we got there, winning the British Open to the World championship in 1995, there were whispers and gossip that it was because I was a manipulative piece of work who had 'bought' every person on the judging panel.

That took the cake.

Whatever it is – dance or TV – I study my craft as if my life depends on it. I live and breathe it. There was no conspiracy other than that. My brain is my most powerful tool.

I have no choice but to work with these people – those frenemies – I just know not to trust them. There are plenty out there who only see you as someone who can provide them with something. They try to be your friend when they want something.

People call me: 'Oh, *Shirley*, I just thought we should catch up because we haven't spoken in such a long time!'

'Nice to hear from you,' I reply, one eyebrow firmly raised. 'How can I help?'

I can normally tell whether they're genuinely calling to see how I am or just trying to get something from me.

And I get that it's very hard for people outside of this world to understand it. I've grown up in it and it's like one big dysfunctional family – and let's face it, all families come with their fair share of issues and bickering. My industry exists in a bubble; we're a small pond and all of us are fishing from that same pool. We see each other all the time and we are in each other's lives whether we want to be or not, so it's all priced in.

But you'll maybe understand a bit better now why I keep my guard up. I've learned over the years that even though I adore most of the students who come to private lessons with me, there are boundaries I have to maintain.

There's a tiny handful who have crossed that line from a teacher-and-student relationship into a real friendship. One young lady, Yulia Musikhina, is in her late thirties now and I'd trust her with my life because she's stuck by me come hell or high water. At one point she was told by certain others that she should leave me and there was a great deal of pressure being placed on her then-young shoulders. Yulia had a conversation with another teacher about the difficult position she was being put in and he asked her if she wanted to leave.

Yulia said no she didn't.

'Don't leave, then,' he advised. 'Don't do it just because somebody else tells you to do something you're not happy with.'

Not only did she stay on as my student, but she shared that whole conversation with me and I think that speaks volumes about her character and integrity.

Attagirl.

While there are not many people in dance that I have absolute faith in, Yulia is one of them. She's like the daughter I never had and is cut from a different cloth because gratitude and loyalty in my industry are very thin on the ground.

It doesn't matter if people want to try out different teachers and leave you for pastures new, that's normal and expected. Situations change, people want to experiment with other methods, we all move on. What I can't get my head around is the double-crossing that goes on in between – at least when Maurizio Vescovo left me, he said it to my face.

Down-to-earth, grounded people who just get on with the job and aren't interested in stirring the pot or inserting themselves into the centre of a drama are scarce in dance. Just when you feel you have somebody in your corner, they'll do something to show that they never gave a stuff about you, and I'm wise now to the fair-weather phonies who smile to your face but sharpen the dagger behind your back.

I'm a tough nut, but I'm far happier with my small yet perfectly formed inner circle – the vast majority of people in my life simply don't make the cut. I find a whole lot more value in those most-trusted connections than I ever would in a larger group who didn't fully have my back.

'Trust is earned, respect is given, and loyalty is demonstrated. Betrayal of any one of those is to lose all three.'

ZIAD K. ABDELNOUR

Even those closest to you can heel-turn on you when you least expect it. I mentioned earlier that just before I made my *Strictly* debut, Corky gave an interview to the *Sun* newspaper which was so brutal that I find it difficult to do justice to the impact it had. It was grotesque.

It also happened to be around my mother's 80th birthday and took some of the shine away from what should have been a time of celebration.

The piece landed the week before the *Strictly* launch and I was already a bag of nerves about everything that lay ahead – my publicist at the time wasn't given a heads-up that the article was running so we were all blindsided by it.

And when I saw the front page featuring a photo of me holding a judge's paddle displaying the number ten alongside a headline declaring *that* as the number of lovers I'd taken during my marriage to Corky, I was almost physically sick.

It was all lies, so unforgiving. It felt like a violation and there were a lot of tears.

It was also a lesson in how fast people come out of the woodwork when there's a claim to fame and a couple of grand up for grabs. Everyone suddenly wants to tell their story and see you fall flat on your arse.

I don't know why he did it. I'm not even sure Corky knew why. Maybe the journalist had caught him at a weak moment.

Whatever the motivation, it took me a long time to recover from that breach of trust and there was a point when I didn't think I'd be able to speak to him again.

It felt like a bridge too far to come back from.

However, dust settles, things move on and the heart (well, my heart at least) manages to forgive. There is so much history between Corky and me, and because of our son and now our grandson, he is always going to be in my life. So for their sake, I have managed to find a way to forge ahead.

I've forgiven for my own sake, too. Forgiveness is part of letting go and holding on to something so heavy puts you at risk of being dragged down into that dark hole of bleakness. I've been there a few times and don't ever want to go back.

What Corky did was painful, but I won't carry it. At least he said I was a good dancer and teacher, so there was a compliment buried in among the insults and untruths.

While we might have been hopeless at being married to each other, parenting-wise, we've always been a good team and now we have a grandson together and Banksi has been very healing.

Don't we all have flaws?

When it comes to connection, history counts for a lot more than we perhaps realise until those bonds are put to the test. Take me and Sammy Stopford, for example. We've fallen out over the years and driven each other bonkers, but we have these unbelievably strong roots. Sometimes those roots are as thick and as solid as steel cable and our relationship feels unbreakable.

At other times they've become thin like the flimsiest of cotton threads and there have been occasions when I've thought they were going to snap. Surely too fragile to survive.

But somehow, they remain attached because – subconsciously, at least – neither of us will ever allow the break to happen.

No matter what wedges other people put between me and my past relationships, I know I'll always stay connected to them in one way or another.

There will always be ups, downs, fallouts; we'll be friends, not friends, business partners, not business partners. But there is also always a force – something far bigger than any one of us – pulling us back together.

Sammy has always been good at reading me. I went out to lunch with him not so long ago when I wasn't in a great place mentally. I put on the usual Shirley show of strength: pressed the button, did the thing, had the lunch and thought I'd cracked it.

He called me later.

'You weren't yourself today, young lady,' he said.

Wow.

I found it fascinating the fact Sammy had recognised my inner slump because I'm usually so accomplished at disguising how I'm really feeling. I don't like asking for help or showing any sign of a chink in my armour.

If somebody else needs support, I'm the first on the scene to step in and get them back on their feet. I enjoy being useful and feeling wanted and needed.

But when I need it myself, I worry that people will see it as a sign of weakness, even though I know I'm not weak and I don't think that of anyone else who asks for help.

A lot to unravel there, right?

'Stay away from negative people. They have a problem for every solution.'

ANONYMOUS

I can't talk about trust and connection without going back to the community I grew up in. The place where I first learned what it meant to belong and be part of something and which lay my foundations, shaping the person I am today.

I've been all over the world, but the Leasowe housing estate is the place I will always call home. Some people work their way up and move on from where they started out and want to forget about or even deny the place they came from.

Don't remind me of that, don't talk about that, it's all in the past.

They ignore the fact that all that history and experience is part of what makes you who you are. Something I have always endeavoured to do is maintain my connection to my roots. I always come back to Wallasey and I'm still fiercely proud of it.

There was very little money on that estate, but if someone fell short, everyone was there to help. I learned the importance of looking out for others, checking in on your neighbour, the value in mutual support.

Remembering where you've come from gives you the anchor to keep you grounded and grateful.

Whenever I'm back in Wallasey, I always pay a visit to the Leasowe and take a drive down our old street, Cameron Road. I see where our flat was and the house we moved to which felt like such a big step up.

I see St Chad's church, my old doctor's surgery, the library, the pub, the fish and chip shop.

I see the little playground where we used to play as kids and the street corner where the big red phone box used to sit – it was used by everybody because no one had a landline back then. I see the muddy field we walked across every morning to get to school.

I'll call for lunch at the Lighthouse pub, a place my dad spent so much time in, just down the road in Wallasey Village.

I often wonder what happened to the boy – a neighbour called Danny McGary – who was my first love. I remember I used to look at him and think, 'Oh my gosh, he's so smart, so good-looking,' and being helpless to this developing crush.

And then there was Susan Barrell whose mother Dot used to come and take care of me and David while Mum was out working. Susan often comes down to stay with me in London and it's great to remember the old stories together from our treasured 60-year friendship. She's one in a million and never wants anything, just time to spend with me and to have a good laugh.

I also stay in touch with Irene Hamilton who was my first dance partner and I always enjoy catching up with her. It's those historical ties that are the most special.

There's also something very powerful about female friendship and I'm incredibly lucky to have a great gang of strong women in my life – Terrie Martin, whom I've known for 35 years because our children went to school together, and Karen Hilton and Denise Weavers, whom I grew up with on dance floors across the north of England. They are some of my favourite people in the world.

And I can't forget my gay gaggle, Alan and Nathan Grundy, who have both been by my side through thick and thin. They are family to me in every way.

But here's the catch. Despite our collective decades of friendship, the holidays, the nights out, the crises, the joys and the heartaches we've shared, I still find it hard to let them in completely.

That is not a reflection on them but on me and my baggage. My invisible scars.

It's safer for me to stay cautious.

But all those connections do mean something and I know I'm fortunate to have them. People come and go. Some come for a week, some for a season, some stay for a few years. It doesn't mean they're not relevant. It's just a fact of life and they were there to serve a purpose at that particular time.

If you want to be on my team, good for you. And if you don't, that's OK too. I have great people in my life because I chose them.

Come what may, I will survive.

Shirley's Shimmers

Surround yourself with people who uplift and
inspire you, not those who drain your energy.

✖

Trust your gut – if something feels off about
someone, don't ignore those instincts.

✖

If you feel like you're constantly giving and getting nothing
in return, it's probably time to reassess that relationship.

✖

Quality over quantity – having a small group you trust
completely is better than a large group of fake friends.

✖

Watch out for the people who only show their faces
when they need something but are nowhere to be seen
when *you* do. You are worth more than that.

✖

Actions speak louder than words,
so look at how they treat others.

STEP TEN

Hold Your Frame

RESILIENCE

'Shut your gob
and get on with it.'

AUDREY

*T*o maintain your frame in dance means keeping a solid, intentional posture in your upper body. This allows you to lead or follow in harmony with your partner: no hunching, arching or leaning forward. It's about stability, strength and holding firm.

In a wider sense, it can be about knowing exactly who you are and staying centred no matter what chaos might be unfurling around you.

Coming off the back of my first series of *Strictly* felt like I'd just run a marathon through quicksand. Overnight, the show had catapulted me to household name status and the three months we'd been on air had been an emotionally charged crash course in living in the spotlight.

To put it bluntly, I was knackered. And a bit shell-shocked.

For the first few months of 2018, I didn't quite know who I was any more. I'd become this character on TV who everyone wanted a piece of, caught up in the overwhelm of a fast-paced and ruthless industry where I felt like I was constantly chasing my own tail. The scrutiny felt merciless.

Who could I trust? Who could I talk to? It was all such unfamiliar territory to me. I knew my own industry inside and out, upside down and back to front, but in TV I knew nothing and nobody.

The BBC were a great support during this initial whirlwind and had guided me through the fluctuations of the series, but they were powerless to stop the intrusion which was especially difficult for my mother to cope with. Not only had Corky called her a 'termite' in his hit piece with the *Sun*, accusing her of undermining our marriage, but in subsequent articles, details about David's death had been printed, which was distressing for a woman like Mum who had spent her whole life guarding her privacy as if her very existence depended on it.

Therefore, when I was offered a new contract for the 2018 series, I wasn't sure I could accept it, and my mum and I had a very candid conversation about whether I should continue. Perhaps one season was all I had in me and was all we could withstand as a family.

I told her that if she didn't want me to do it, I'd quit that self-same day.

'Let me think about it,' she said.

The BBC wanted me back. They thought I'd brought something new to the panel, I'd managed to ride out the post-Len Goodman storm and had proved rather popular with the viewers, who had warmed to my northern relatability and been impressed with my dance knowledge.

Despite the external pressures, on screen I'd found my stride. By the end of the series, I felt very much at home in that head judge's chair. I'd enjoyed the challenge of live TV and loved being part of this super-slick operation with a studio full of creative minds, ambition and talent.

But I couldn't give the producers an answer until my mum and I had sat down and chatted at length. And I think that's when we both realised the platform *Strictly* offered for my charity work. If I kept this job, the opportunities it would provide me with to help other people were endless. I could become a voice for those who had no voice.

That flipped my whole perspective. *Strictly* puts me on people's radars in a way no other job can and gives me and my charities the sort of reach and publicity one can only dream of. That appealed to me.

We talked about the impact of the media attention and agreed that it couldn't ever be as intense as that first roller-coaster year – everything was already out there for the world to see and there wasn't much more that could be raked up. Plus, going into my second series, I'd no longer be the newbie, meaning the flurry of interest wouldn't be as extreme.

Weighing up all the pros and cons, eventually, as a family, we chose to hold our nerve and go forward with a second series. It wasn't a decision we took lightly, but we balanced the potential cost to our peace against the opportunity to achieve something greater than that, something that really mattered.

And besides, waving the white flag of surrender has never been part of my playbook and especially not when there's something worth fighting for.

I have never regretted the decision to sign that contract and walk through the fire for *Strictly*, because that show has given me some of the best times of my life and introduced me to so many inspiring and brilliant people, many of whom I'm proud to call my friends.

It has also given me the platform we talked about and I've been able to raise awareness, support and talk about the causes closest to my heart – Suicide & Co, CALM, Alder Hey Hospital, Centrepoint, Macmillan and the RSPCA. I take on as much charity work as I can, always being careful not to spread myself too thin. If I can use my profile to give back to other people then that means the world to me.

'Losing your head in a crisis is a good way to become the crisis.'

C.J. REDWINE

Although I'm now used to dealing with the pressures that come as part and parcel of being on the biggest show on telly, there are still times when my ability to keep calm and carry on is put through its paces.

I do understand the press have a job to do and that *Strictly* is always going to be something the public are interested in reading about, but it's hard to hold my tongue when I see it taking a pummelling across the media. However, nothing and no one – not me, not the celebrities and certainly not the professional dancers – is bigger than the show.

I stay in my lane.

However, *Strictly* is the BBC's jewel in the crown and I feel it should be protected because there is nothing else like it for bringing families together. Grandparents, children, mothers and fathers right across the age and generational spectrum have watched and adored it for more than 20 years.

I cast my mind back to 2020 when we pulled out the stops to put the series on through all the Covid restrictions and it really felt that we were able to bring some joy to the country during that anguished period. Immediately before that year's final on 19 December, the then Prime Minister Boris Johnson announced new rules which would mean many Christmas plans had to be cancelled and we all felt an enormous sense of duty to lift the nation's spirits that night.

Strictly is part of Britain's cultural identity and the prospect of it no longer existing is unthinkable. There are always people who want to pull it down, but if they ever took it off air, there's nothing that could possibly replace it.

The show has survived many challenges and continues to produce the goods – last year was one of our most successful series with nearly ten million tuning in for the highest-scoring final ever and that, I think, speaks volumes.

Sometimes the strongest move you can make is to keep your cool, anchor down and hold the line. What's meant to rise will find a way.

'The secret of life is to fall seven times and to get up eight.'

PAULO COELHO

Everything that's worth knowing, I've learned through failure. Getting to the top of our game and winning the British Open to the World championship in 1983 had been relatively straightforward with Sammy, but it was the hard push with Corky, the setbacks, the tears and the mountains we had to climb which taught me the most.

Failure doesn't flatter you like success can and does. It asks difficult questions, shapes character and breeds courage. It helps you learn that with absolute dedication to the cause and a steadfast refusal to countenance those who try to drag you down, you can get there.

Staying committed to your goals is a choice. Some people are born like that; they have doors continually slammed in their face, they're pushed down and pushed out, but they keep coming back.

Others learn to be that way through circumstance; they have to find that steely core in order to survive. That's the camp I fall into. There were plenty of times when I felt like giving up on the quest to help Corky become a champ, but I never would have and never did. Quitters never win and winners never quit. Sore losers achieve very little in life – they become trapped in a cycle of self-pity rather than analysing what might have gone wrong and putting plans in place to make sure it doesn't happen again.

Take all knocks with good grace. Have a cry in your bedroom and get over yourself – don't air your dirty laundry in public.

I've told you all about my mother's fortitude and how her strength of character influenced me, but I should point out that both my husbands also played a big part in teaching me about resilience.

They were brimming with the stuff.

I swear to God, Sammy could survive an atomic bomb. He's probably the strongest person I know. And then there's Corky, who made it to the top of an industry where he was the punch-line to every bad joke for so many years – while I didn't fully appreciate it at the time, when I step back now and look at what he withstood, I have to applaud him.

'Stick with me, Shirley,' he'd say, 'I'm going to take you places.'

I was the one pulling the strings, but that was his stock line and when you're around that sort of hubris 24/7, it gets into your head too. I knew that everyone thought my plan to make him a champion was a colossal waste of time, but all that disdain and derision teaches you to be ironclad.

I was interviewed before that 1995 British Open to the World final and they asked me what I was expecting from the night.

'I'm not leaving without that trophy,' I replied without hesitation, meaning every word and putting that energy out there – the same persistence which has been a running theme throughout my life. There's a clear link back to the attitude I had at 17 when I told Simon Byrne at Parsons & Whittemore Lyddon Limited that I wasn't leaving his office without a job.

What I didn't ever want to do was look back on my life and wish that I'd tried a bit harder or pushed myself a little further and be left wondering about what might have been.

Coulda, shoulda, woulda.

That's why I'm always striving to be better than I was before. Even now I study books about technique and scour them for different ways to teach and pass on my knowledge, searching outside the box, never quite sure what I'm going to find but always looking.

If I'm teaching one way and I discover something better, I'll switch it up.

Staying curious means I never get stale and as long as I'm learning, I'm succeeding. And I know not to be afraid of missing the mark or of so-called 'failure' because it's always the recovery that produces the greatest lesson.

'I do not try to dance better than anyone else. I only try to dance better than myself.'

MIKHAIL BARYSHNIKOV

Just because the wind is blowing in a certain direction, you don't need to be swept along with the breeze. True strength and contentment means finding your own path, so I won't follow the crowd or conform for convenience.

That's often the easiest option, but I dance to the beat of my own drum.

I haven't always been as single-minded and there have been times when I've caved in to pressure and allowed myself to be influenced or even frightened into doing things purely to satisfy other people.

I remember once booking some lessons with a Norwegian dancer called Espen Salberg, who Sammy and I had come second to in the British Open to the Worlds back in 1982. Espen and his partner Kirsten had retired straight after that victory which paved the way for our win the following year and, although I didn't know it, what would be the beginning of the end for the Non-stop Stopfords.

I wanted to go to Espen to train with Corky because I knew he was a top-notch teacher who could do great things for us and push us onto the next level, but for all sorts of ridiculous internal political reasons, another big name in the industry got very irate at this prospect.

To my eternal shame, I fell into line and did as I was told, cancelling all the lessons I'd booked with Espen, which meant we never got to train with him. It's a decision I've regretted ever since because we missed out on experiencing the benefit of his knowledge and talent.

And for what? To keep other people happy? So's not to rock the boat?

I should have stood my ground and resisted being strong-armed into a decision that wasn't mine. I'd been weak.

So, when Ruud Vermeij came aboard Team Ballas in the early nineties to the sneers of virtually everyone else around us, I resolved not to make the same mistake twice.

This time I stood up.

For me, Ruud is a genius. He has studied psychotherapy and has a doctorate in Movement and Dance Studies, but there were plenty who didn't appreciate his credentials and only focused on the fact he'd never hit the big time as a dancer himself.

When I met him by chance in Japan, travelling on a bus between events, we hit it off immediately and spent the whole six-hour journey deep in conversation. Everything he said about how he understood the mind to work, the sensitivity zones on the female body and many other things besides made perfect sense to me and he explained it all in such a way that I could visualise it. I'd never heard anyone articulate things so clearly.

I thought, 'I've got to work with this man.'

He came into my life for a reason and Ruud was a pivotal person in terms of me finding the courage to pursue the mission with Corky and to win – twice – when everyone else was telling us we were hopeless. Ruud never told us that. Ever.

He put up with our fighting and petty squabbles, all our paddies and tantrums, and he gave me more tools for dance and life in general than I could have ever imagined.

'Let's push your strengths and hide your weaknesses,' he'd say.

That's what Ruud was all about: simple, sound advice. He's since written a book and said that he learned a lot from us about how to train future generations, which was a very generous accolade.

We're still friends – he works as a therapist, still teaches ballroom dancing, is one of the busiest people I know and probably the cleverest I've ever met in my entire dance journey.

Ruud is now widely regarded as one of the best coaches in the world, having produced many a ballroom champion in the decades since he took on me and Corky.

Which proves I was right to stand firm and trust my judgement. If something feels right to you, don't wait for permission or look for consensus. Ignore the mob and back yourself.

'Life's challenges are not supposed to paralyse you, they're supposed to help you discover who you are.'

BERNICE JOHNSON REAGON

I'm just going to come out and say it. I know it's probably highly controversial and might well ruffle a few feathers, but I have to tell it how I see it.

The younger generation of today seem so much less resilient than in years gone by and I think we need to look at what might be going on. Millennials and Gen Zs are often seen by us 'Boomers' as being too sensitive and easily offended – they've been nicknamed Generation Snowflake, which seems a little harsh but contains an element of truth.

Before that puts anyone's nose out of joint, I recognise I'm making a big generalisation. I know plenty of under-35s who are tougher than a two-dollar steak and will always put up and show up.

However, I have a strong sense that a lot of kids at the moment veer towards entitled and expect everything to land in their lap. They don't want to fight or struggle to achieve. They don't want to have to communicate or interact and too many of them wouldn't say boo to a goose. I come across so many now who act as if the sky has fallen in if someone says the 'wrong' thing.

The obsession with social media and living life online seems to have made the generations who have grown up on technology too reliant on the opinions of others and too willing to be led, instead of using those different points of view as a map and navigating it on their own.

One of the most important lessons we can teach our young people is how to find it within themselves to make independent choices. As their elders, we can guide and advise, but when it comes to the crunch, they have to make their own decisions (and their own mistakes) and then live or die by whatever happens.

Shielding the younger generations from any discomfort and solving every problem for them denies them the chance to build resilience which, heaven knows, they're going to need in this world.

When I think of my grandson, I want him to learn how to run a bank account and how to save. I want to make sure that he is street-smart and can hold a conversation. I'm always advising the young kids I teach to make sure not to spend more than they earn: pay off your bills, be as debt-free as you can and this will give you peace of mind. Life skills – all of which are just as important as being able to point out where Canada is on a map.

I know this is a challenging era to be growing up in and you couldn't pay me to go back to being a young woman in this day and age. The pressures to look a certain way have never been greater, the compare-and-despair culture is entrenched and the world feels more unstable and unpredictable than I can ever remember.

But we must help our children become emotionally resilient and equip them with a strong sense of self in order to cope with all of that.

We've got to stop wrapping them up in cotton wool because that's not doing them any favours.

'You gain strength, courage, and confidence by every experience in which you really stop to look fear in the face.'

ELEANOR ROOSEVELT

In among the hustle and bustle backstage before a competition is one of my favourite places to be. Give me Blackpool and the smell of Bengay muscle rub over a beach in Barbados any day.

The panic of a last-minute crisis because somebody's hair won't stay put or they've forgotten their safety pins for their numbers.

Tension you could cut with a knife.

Bodies crowded into the same tiny space trying to get changed, limber up and shake off the pre-competition nerves.

Even after all these years I still love being in the thick of every bit of it.

Everyone has their own rituals and way of conducting themselves before the competition begins. Mine was pushing the buckle on my T-bar shoe strap inwards until it hit the middle. Some people like to disappear from the hullabaloo entirely – the nine-times UK champion and World Latin American winner Joanna Leunis and her partner would always take themselves off to a small quiet corner where nobody else was. You wouldn't see hide nor hair of them until it was time for them to take the floor.

The atmosphere and energy makes your heart race and gives you rush after rush of endorphins, like you're just about to enter a Roman arena where gladiators come face to face with prowling tigers. It's survival of the fittest.

It's a tantalising dynamic because everybody trains with the same teachers and will be judged by the people who have taught them. What's important is that the judging panels are balanced fairly because the truth is, my industry is a mess at the moment and I fear for its future. We've had a split of the societies that oversee the competitions – it's one organisation against another and everybody is trying to demand which 'side' people should be taking. In my opinion, no one should be telling anybody where they should be dancing.

The conflict revolves around differing views on various rules and regulations, but I have always refused to pick a side because as far as I'm concerned, they're all as bad as each other. I'm going to train my kids regardless of the sniping that's going on around us.

I tell the boys and girls to hold their nerve because I've got young dancers who are anxious, stressed and scared out of their wits from the pressure coming at them to make a choice. They're being backed into making rock-and-hard-place decisions that could affect their whole future. I've seen messages from professionals written to younger couples saying, 'How dare you have a lesson with this person, they are trash and I'll never teach you again.'

Or, for example, 'Why are you only booking two lessons with me? You should be booking four, I'm your main teacher.'

That's what we're dealing with here, people with power and influence throwing their weight around and trying to draw lines, even telling dancers that they won't mark them if they go to one side and vice versa.

Threats, bullying, abuse.

It's like playing chess where you've got to be three moves ahead of the opposition all the time and whatever you do, you don't want to be the pawn.

The kings and queens are dictating the play.

'You dance where you want to dance and you stand strong,' I say. 'Don't let anyone tell you that you have to be in one camp or another, don't let anyone threaten you.'

I'm so exasperated with it all that it makes me want to weep. I can't do anything except expose and push back against it, but I'm not sure it can or will ever change. Things will probably splinter off even further into different pockets of different societies.

That's why I love the United Kingdom Championships in Bournemouth and the International Championships in London, both dance festivals that are run by Christopher and Robin Short who give all of that nonsense no quarter. They put a huge amount of work into making their judging panels neutral and they're fully committed to running contests which are as clean as possible with no room for bias or corruption.

As a result they always get the right winners, in my opinion.

I'd love certain people in my industry to understand that when somebody pays them money for a lesson, they are paying to learn to dance. They're not paying to be bullied or preached at and if they don't want to dance in this competition for one organisation or in that competition for another, it's not the job of the teacher to convince them either way.

STOP DOING IT. Give these young people a great private lesson, quit pushing your politics and don't make your fight their fight. I want people to have freedom to do what they want and spend their money on the teacher they wish to be taught by.

'It's your money, you spend it where you like,' I say.

The more I've learned about what's happening, the more I've tried to educate the younger generation and teach them how to have the courage to reject it.

And, by the way, I don't do this during their paid-for private lessons. That's too expensive. What my students always get from me is the full 45 minutes and if they've got a separate issue they need help with, I do that off the clock. When I'm in the studio, I only work on dancing and I'll talk to them about anything else in my own time. Take me for a cup of coffee and we'll chat for as long as you like, it's a lot cheaper! That's giving back.

As one of the elders in our industry, I see it as my responsibility to follow up on the mental wellbeing of the youngsters who are struggling. There is some duty of care, but no helpline or place to go for emotional support, and we are crying out for something like that – it should be available 52 weeks of the year and funded by the dance industry. In the meantime, I've made it my mission to check in on how people are doing because my students are more than just a private lesson to me.

Not that I want to pamper people – they've still got to grow up in an industry where a strong character counts for a lot – but I never had that cloak around me when I was younger and perhaps I could have done with one.

We need systemic change, but in the meantime I'll make sure that nobody ever walks out of my door feeling they've got no one to talk to and show them how to remain robust and maintain integrity in the face of wicked behaviour.

When people are dreadful, don't be reduced to their level. It's their issue, not yours. And nothing winds a bully up more than seeing their attempts at intimidation being met with a smile. Power dwindles when it's no longer feared.

Shirley's Shimmers

If you need to step back from a situation to protect your
peace, do so. Refocus and return with a clear head.

✗

It's OK to feel overwhelmed but also important to work
through those feelings and find a way to move forward.

✗

Don't give up at the first hurdle; take your time to reflect
and reach a decision on how to move forward.
Knee-jerk reactions rarely bear fruit.

✗

If you are clear about your beliefs and your reasons, stand your
ground, maintain your integrity and don't be swayed or gaslit.

✗

Embrace discomfort from time to time. Find the inner
strength you need to stay calm under pressure.

Dance Like Nobody's Watching

LIBERATION

'Who cares what
other people think?'
AUDREY

*I*magine being able to breeze through life genuinely not giving two hoots about what other people think of you. Think of the freedom that indifference would give you, how much lighter you'd feel, the energy you'd save.

What a gift.

That's what being able to dance like no one is watching means to me. It's giving up on the endless chase for validation and living life as you choose to without worrying about being liked or approved of or held up to other people's expectations.

I know a few people like that, who aren't shackled by the opinions of others, and they are some of the happiest souls I've come across.

My fellow *Strictly* judge Craig Revel Horwood is one. I love that man – he is devil-may-care to his core and he has taught me a lot about the art of not giving a damn. Whatever they throw at him falls on deaf ears – he is literally unflappable – and so when I'm looking at the latest barrage of abuse hurled in my direction because a few people dislike my dress or think I need to lose weight, I ask myself: 'What would Craig do?'

Without fail, the answer to that question is always he wouldn't give a flying you-know-what and so, I tell myself, neither should I.

Not caring – or, at least, caring less – is something I'm getting much better at, although it's quite a test of the mettle when you're in the limelight. Even a tiny bit of fame makes you a target and some people think they're entitled to have a pop because they deem you to be public property. And thanks to the internet, those people have an unregulated Wild West of a platform on which to spout their venom. Blocking out that noise ain't easy.

My introduction to social media and all its toxic glory was a baptism of fire. Before I began on *Strictly*, I wasn't clued up on it in the slightest and didn't even use my phone for emails – they were all sent and received on a computer and my mobile was only for texting and calling.

But, love it or loathe it, part of being in the public eye these days is having a presence on social media and so I had a lot to learn. Fast.

What an eye-opener. I never realised how petty, vile and abusive perfect strangers could be until I started building up a profile on Twitter (now X) and Instagram. Right from the off, I was threatened, insulted and attacked – trolled because people didn't think I was good enough or attractive enough or clever enough.

For the first few weeks of my debut series in 2017 I was deluged with posts on my feeds calling for the Beeb to bring back Len Goodman. They'd draw little coffins and put me inside, make terrible comments about my appearance and taunt me about my 'bingo wings' and my weight.

'Hide your arms, you're too fat, your teeth are false, you're fake.'

'Don't ever wear a halterneck dress again, Shirley, look at your bingo wings you make me feel physically sick.'

'Fire the bitch, she doesn't know what she's talking about.'

'Your hair is a mess. Your face isn't right. What's that mole on your chin? Why don't you get it removed?'

That charmer of a comment took me right back to some of my darkest days as a dancer when I was constantly humiliated about my chin mole and someone, who shall remain nameless, once told me to go out onto the street and have it 'chewed off by a rat'.

I thought I'd heard it all in dance, an industry with no time for sensitive wallflowers, but the level of vitriol being unleashed on my socials was a shock to the system and made me question why I was putting myself out there as a human dartboard. I'd dread turning on my phone at the end of each show and seeing the latest round of verbal assaults come flooding in.

And it wasn't just confined to online. In 2019, I received a hand-delivered letter to the theatre in Darlington where I was appearing in panto telling me how ugly and useless I was and that I should be booted off *Strictly*.

'You might think you're good at your game,' it said, 'but we all know you're shit.'

I kept that letter for many years before eventually ripping it up, although it remains in one of my many Pandora's boxes. Can't help that.

Alongside the press intrusion, the relentless trolling was another factor which made me seriously consider quitting after one season on the show. Although I ultimately decided to plough on, the attacks from the keyboard warriors kept coming and would gain momentum throughout each series. They seemed emboldened by each other and I'd fixate on the very worst of the jibes.

People would tell me to ignore it, but for three months of the year when *Strictly* was on air, it would feel like I was drowning.

It was in 2022 that the vilification hit its peak and I knew something was going to have to give. Funnily enough, that particular series of *Strictly* was one of the most joyful I'd had the privilege of being part of so far – the standard of dancing from the celebrities was astonishingly high. We saw the fabulous Hamza Yassin take the glitter ball trophy with his professional partner Jowita Przystał after a heart-stopping final which left me speechless.

However, away from the cameras the online attacks against me had intensified like never before and the emotional toll it took was not good.

If I wasn't being accused of underscoring contestants, I was being criticised for the way I looked and you'd have to be made of titanium not to feel the impact. It felt like I'd lost control of a situation which was now spiralling. I'm not going to blame it solely on the trolling because there were other things going on simultaneously, but life was starting to feel overwhelming and I didn't know who could help me. It was as if I didn't have anywhere to turn.

There was one especially unpleasant comment which I reposted with the offender's @ handle still visible which then caused my supporters to turn on him. That clearly wasn't the outcome I'd intended – my aim had been to show people the sort of disgusting remarks I was fielding on a daily basis.

But what's good for the goose is good for the gander, right? Wrong.

The man in question got in touch with one of my management team to complain about me and, to add insult to injury, I was then given a dressing down by them as if I was the one who was out of order. This guy was able to do it to me, yet I wasn't able to retaliate or respond.

Make it make sense!

In the end I agreed to take my post down and I spoke to the man on the phone to smooth things over and so we could better understand each other, but I'll never forget that no manager, no publicist, can make you feel safe.

After that, I found Harry, a social media whiz, and hired him to come on board and take over that side of things. By that stage, I didn't want any part of it. Knowing Harry was managing my accounts so that I was still putting out content but didn't have to face the abuse was like being freed.

I only wish I'd done it sooner.

'Don't waste your energy trying to change opinions. Do your thing, and don't care if they like it.'

TINA FEY

With the benefit of being one step removed from it, what I've come to understand about this social media business is that if people choose to be odious, that's a them problem. Not a me problem.

For many years I took it extremely personally, but I refuse to do that any more. I realise it's not a reflection on me and I'm secure enough in myself to know I'm a good person with good morals and intentions and these trolls won't ever shake that.

I have to keep reminding myself that this is a mere smattering of people. For every ten who don't like me, there are a thousand who do. It's not the entire nation dogpiling on me even if it feels like that in the moment.

I know the drill by now and it's entirely predictable. If I ever send a man home, it's because I hate men. If I ever send a woman home, it's because I hate women.

As head judge, I have the casting vote and whoever I choose to let go will be someone's favourite. But while most people are able to shrug their shoulders because they understand that it's a TV show and there can only be one winner, there will always be a handful of hotheads who get on social media and go on the attack.

Part of me gets it. When people become invested in the show and they see the couple they're supporting putting in the hard yards only to have their little hearts broken, it's upsetting.

It is for us on the panel, too! It's always sad when we have to say goodbye; I don't want to send anyone home and especially not when we know how hard they're working and how much they want this. They're all marvellous, but unfortunately somebody has to go.

And still it continues. I'm pretty much unshockable now but the backlash after I eliminated Shayne Ward and his partner

Nancy Xu over Wynne Evans and Katya Jones from the dance-off in 2024 took even me by surprise.

It was the week before we went to Blackpool and so the stakes were high because everyone is desperate to make it to the famous Tower Ballroom. It was going to be gutting for whoever left that week.

But people went to the trouble of organising a petition to get me fired, claiming that I hadn't even bothered trying to conceal my 'blatant favouritism'. It wasn't fair on the other contestants, they said, and it was time for the BBC to cut me loose.

In the end I couldn't resist replying to one of the ringleaders. 'Where do I sign?' I enquired of their petition.

That took the wind out of their sails. These people have no comeback if you laugh at yourself and it's a good way of signalling that this stuff no longer gets to me. Approach it with humour, kill it with wit. I won't give them the satisfaction of thinking they've negatively affected one minute of my day.

Sometimes I'll pop up in the comments on my feed and say, 'You don't know me and I'm sad that you feel like that, but I hope you have a lovely day,' and more often than not, those people will proceed to fall over themselves to apologise.

It all feels very alienating when you're being subjected to what feels like a daily beating, but I've reached a point where I won't bow down to it. Neither do I condemn these people to the block button straight away – I try to give keyboard warriors a second chance, especially now I've worked a lot with mental illness because I think their posts must be a symptom of something else. I don't know what they're going through in their life that's made them reach out and be so mean – maybe battering me makes them feel momentarily better about themselves. Maybe they haven't had a good day and they're lashing out. Maybe they've experienced a failure or have just received bad news. I try to hold some empathy for them even if it means that, hey ho, I'll become their punchbag for a while.

I guess it can make people feel they're big and important for five minutes, like they're Charlie Big Potatoes. It gives them this false sense of security and delusions of grandeur.

So, they get a couple of chances but by the third time they're blocked and after that I won't see them ever again. Goodbye, sayonara, on yer bike!

And, just to be clear, I dish out instant blocks for men who have the temerity to send me pictures of their willy because that still happens from time to time and I have no desire to see some bloke's old rucksack dangling down between his legs.

I know I say don't judge, but those guys? I find myself reaching for my 'two' paddle …

So, while I'm much better at handling the hate these days, I haven't quite achieved the Craig Revel Horwood gold standard of DGAF energy. I know I should pay no heed to it and people say don't read it, but I do. Of course I do.

If you give me a load of positive, complimentary messages, I'll still manage to find the one that's rude and I find it sad that we now live in a world where some of us are so needlessly cruel.

But I do look for the tin suit Corky Ballas gave to me. If I put that on, the bullets hurt but they don't penetrate. I won't let them win – when people want to see you fall, that's all the more reason to stand tall.

Imagine your ears as the doors to your home. Mine are red with a big number six on the front. You don't need to open them and let all the negative people in. If you want to keep your mind clean and tidy and beautiful so that you can sleep at night, just keep the doors closed.

Has social media made people more judgemental and vitriolic? For sure.

But it's just thoughtless words by faceless cowards. We need to remind ourselves that there are people – real-life people – who love and support us and they are the ones who deserve our attention.

'Mistakes are part of the dues one pays for a full life.'

SOPHIA LOREN

Part of my bumpy road towards caring less has been to start embracing the cock-ups. For so long I've been focused on perfection to the detriment of everything else, including my own mental health.

I used to be so tough on myself, but the fear of making a mistake and allowing that fear to control my choices was the biggest mistake of all. Whether it's in the choreography or on the dance floor of life itself, dropping the ball is OK, just as long as you own it, keep moving on and don't let it define your worth.

In one of our recent Dance With Us sessions, when I was demonstrating the routine, I messed up, forgetting a tiny section of steps in front of all our paying customers. At one time, not so long ago, that would have taken two days of beating myself up for me to get over. And even then it would have continued to haunt me at inopportune moments for weeks and months to come.

That day, I went with the flow, quickly recovered, most of the class were none the wiser, Vito and I carried on with our session and I enjoyed the rest of my day. I've honestly not thought about it again until now.

I don't enjoy tripping up, but I also know there's no such thing as perfection, so I've ditched that futile quest and replaced it with an intention to be all that I can be today.

What is 'perfect' anyway? It's infinity and beyond and you're never, ever going to get there because no matter what you do, there'll always be some fly in the ointment.

Like my good friend Ruud says, push your strengths and hide your weaknesses.

I've also let go of what used to be a chronic need to people-please, which I can see now is just way too much hassle. All that walking on eggshells to keep the peace, the bending and flexing I've performed to earn acceptance and to be loved. I'm through with all that.

I no longer need nor seek other people's approval and from now on, I'm not going to spend time trying to convince anyone to give me the benefit of the doubt.

If you like me, you like me. If you don't, you don't.

Neither am I going to concern myself over what people say behind my back. I generally find out because most people love a gossip so it usually gets back to me – that's quite a powerful position, but none of it touches me.

I'd been teaching a young Latin couple who also recently had a lesson with another female coach and she'd used the time she had with them to carry out a character assassination on me. She told them I'd never danced with feeling, I wasn't a good person and hadn't ever been a great dancer. They were paying to hear that claptrap and then they came back and shared everything with me.

My reaction was to do precisely nothing because it didn't faze me even for a second. I certainly wasn't going to expend any energy going off like a bat out of hell at the woman who had been running her mouth about me. I wasn't going to let her words impinge on my peace of mind either.

The only response I felt was frustration on my couple's behalf because they'd paid her good money for her to waste the session with a diatribe.

I just put it in a box, shelved it and made a mental note. Another one not to be trusted.

There's a quiet kind of power that comes from no longer fretting about fitting in and kicking the desire to be universally liked. If someone wants to trash talk about me, go right ahead. I'm not going to be everyone's cup of tea and that's OK. People have chip-chipped away at me since forever – little digs here, a negative comment there.

But I am secure in myself, who I am and what I've achieved, and resolute in my dedication to giving my students the best I have.

When I think of the emotional labour I've spent worrying about what everyone thought, I'm not sure whether to laugh or cry.

Be yourself, stick to your guns and to hell with anyone who tries to bring you down. From now on, the only person I'm going to please is myself.

'Be yourself; everyone else is already taken.'

ATTRIBUTED TO OSCAR WILDE

We live in a society where, as women get older, the more we're told what is and isn't 'age-appropriate'.

Give me a break.

Even friends of mine tell me I can't do this or say that or wear that dress because it's not 'age-appropriate' and I thank them for their input and go ahead and do what the hell I want anyway. I think *that* is an attitude befitting of my years!

I've started to think more about how I see myself in a way I've never really done before. I love that I can forgive. I love that I'm family oriented. I love that I've been blessed with a positive energy, a kind heart and a bubbly personality.

I love that I stay as true to myself as I possibly can, that I don't have to agree with somebody else if I don't want to and don't have to do anything I don't want to do at my age. I'm only going to do what fits and feels right for me, and I'm going to make those choices myself without the help of other people, with the exception of my son whom I will always listen to.

I love that I can stand up for myself and how protective I am of the people I care about the most. I love that I have empathy and really *feel* what others are going through. I'm over-the-top generous, to the point of almost giving everything I have away.

I also love that God gave me dainty feet and a beautifully shaped pair of ankles which are perfect for Rumba walks.

I love that I can laugh at myself – if I was a big-headed person, I would never have come out dressed as Miss Trunchbull for the *Strictly* musicals week in 2024. I remember Motsi looked at me in abject horror with my makeup-free face, severe bun and padded suit and said, 'I could never do that, Shirls. I don't know how you can.' We both had a good giggle, though.

But it's all part of the theatre, isn't it? I enjoy always giving things a go, pushing myself front and centre and delivering that little bit extra.

When I sat down to start writing this book, I was looking back at all the TV shows I'd done over the last few years from *Cooking with the Stars* to the prestigious CBeebies *Bedtime Stories* and for the first time I thought, 'Good for you, Shirley.'

I like that I can be full of surprises. People are often shocked to find out that my backside is covered in tattoos. Yes, really! All of them represent something significant to me – I have butterflies to symbolise freedom, a frog because my brother loved them and we've collected them ever since he died, a ladybird for my mother, I have Mark's name there and I also had Danny's inked in the middle of my back … Oops!

That wasn't one of my wisest decisions, granted. I'm going to have to get that covered up now. Any suggestions? Let me know.

I don't really talk about them or show them off, mostly because of where they are (!) but also because they are so personal to me. My son loves tattoos and his body is a work of genius art – arms, back, legs … he's covered. I used to hate tattoos on him but I can see my thoughts were being influenced by my mother on that front. I've noticed that I've been swayed by her likes and dislikes throughout my life and so Mark's body art doesn't bother me at all now – it's his life and I respect that. You do what's good for you and let me do what's good for me.

Once you start thinking that way, it's very freeing.

I will always care about how other people feel but only those who really matter to me. I care about what my family think. I care about the feelings of my friends and the colleagues I love. But not the figureheads in the dance industry who are power hungry and driven by envy. And not random social media trolls either.

Instead, I will use their comments as fuel to propel me forward. Their hate will only succeed in making me shine brighter, to continue blazing my own trail.

To dance like no one's watching.

To embrace the freedom to be me.

Shirley's Shimmers

Your worth is not dependent on other people's validation.

✗

Not everyone is going to like you. That's OK!
Spend your time and engage with the people who do.

✗

Remember that confident, happy, secure people
don't spend their time being hateful towards
other humans online. Don't allow faceless
internet trolls to drag you down to their level.

✗

Striving for perfection is like chasing a
moving target – it will always elude you.

✗

Someone else's opinion of you is none of your business.

✗

Life is truly beautiful when you stop caring about getting every
step right – if you stumble in your Samba or jumble up your
Jive, pick yourself up and get back on the dance floor.

STEP TWELVE

Be the Choreographer

EMPOWERMENT

'If you own the story, you get to write the ending.'

AUDREY

*T*he greatest choreographers in the world have vision, imagination and creativity in abundance. They are architects who are unafraid to push boundaries and they instinctively know how to tell a story and express emotion through movement.

They are skilled in communication and when they talk, dancers sit up and listen.

Choreographers call the shots.

Being your own choreographer means taking ownership of your personal story, setting your rhythm and choosing the steps, which is exactly what I've been doing myself over most of my years. At my age now, I feel I have more control over my life than ever before.

For the first time, I'm in the driver's seat. There are no back-seat passengers trying to give me directions or take over the wheel. It's just me and the open road.

I'm financially stable and don't owe a penny to anybody, which makes me independent and free – I've built this life myself, brick by brick, and I'm now at the point where if something doesn't serve me or is causing me worry, I will kiss it goodbye.

I've found the confidence to speak out about the rotten apples in my industry and I don't worry about who that upsets any more because I know the truth is what counts.

I make my own choices and those decisions will centre around what is my best for the people I keep close.

I have high expectations of those who work for me, but am twice as tough on myself. If things fall apart, that's on me because the fish stinks from the head down. I'm at the top and so when something goes wrong, I'm accountable.

I've also discovered that the most empowering word in the English language is 'no'. I'm too long in the tooth to have to deal with divas and disrespect. I choose how I spend my time, where I place my energy and how I protect my peace and I'm able to do that because these days I make most of my decisions with my head.

For too long I allowed my heart to dictate, but it's been hurt so many times and holds on to a lot of pain which can muddle my judgement. My head, thankfully, is pretty clear and I can generally rely on it to know what's right.

The main reason I'm in such a strong position today, where I'm able to run the show, picking and choosing the jobs I take on rather than feeling obliged to accept them, is because of the years of groundwork I've put in. Always showing up even when things were tough, learning from my mistakes and staying consistent.

Earlier this year, producers gave me one day off the *Strictly* tour to go and judge the United Kingdom championship, which meant travelling 250 miles through the night from Sheffield down to Bournemouth, grabbing a quick nap in the back of the car en route, arriving on the south coast at 5am, doing a quick change, hair and makeup and then being in my judging chair by nine.

I finished the day at 11pm and got back in the car to drive all the way to Newcastle where we were doing two shows – a matinee and an evening – the following day.

I didn't blink, it was just what needed to be done. I set my own standards, so I'll always be the first one in the car or through the door. It's very rare that I'm late – if the call time is 8am, I see it as my responsibility to be there 30 minutes before. If you're turning up exactly on the hour, then you're neither early nor prepared, and if you're arriving late, there's a knock-on effect to everyone else's day all because one person hasn't bothered to be on time.

I can't be doing with that sort of entitled behaviour and just assuming other people will fall into line while you suit yourself. Timekeeping is everything for me and it was my mother I learned that from. If she said she was putting dinner on the table at 4pm because she was dashing out to her second job, David and I knew we needed to be there promptly. Her whole life worked to a schedule and we had to conform to that otherwise we wouldn't have functioned as a household.

When I did *Who Do You Think You Are?*, I learned that same discipline stretched back generations. My relatives worked in the wash house – I haven't descended from royalty or aristocracy; we come from cotton stock and every one of us toiled to earn a living.

So maybe it's part of my DNA – to me it certainly feels innate. I've passed it on to my son and hopefully he'll have passed it on to his son too, because there's nothing better in life than working hard to pay your way and creating a world where you have earned the right to decide where you want to go.

It's that discipline which will spur you on. I've known great dancers with a huge amount of flexibility and fluidity who never made it in the industry because they didn't have the drive or the brain cells to push it.

There are many people who perhaps aren't as naturally gifted as others or who face other challenges, but their work ethic trumps everyone else's and that has sent them to the top.

Look no further than our fabulous 2024 *Strictly* winner Chris McCausland and how he never gave up. I reckon at the beginning he'd thought he wasn't going to get past week two, but when he did, something switched. He gave it some welly all the way through and the nation got it absolutely right by crowning him champion – it wasn't just about his dancing, because everybody in that final was a great dancer; it was about true resilience, a determination to figure out a way to make it work and that infectious sense of humour.

Chris didn't want the sob story or the sympathy vote and we can all learn lessons from his *Strictly* journey. It was his perseverance and commitment to the cause which captured my heart too.

If you make yourself memorable, you will always stand out. That's what I tried to do when I came back with Corky. People didn't have to say we were the best, but as long as they recognised our will to win and the fact we grafted harder than anybody else, that's what mattered to me.

It's where a lot of people go wrong in today's society. They think it's all about the straight leg, the turned-out foot, the intricate footwork, but it's so much deeper than that.

That word lucky? I won't have it said to me. I'm not lucky. I just worked hard.

> *'If you want to be the best, you have to do things that other people aren't willing to do.'*
>
> MICHAEL PHELPS

When I'm committed to something, I don't allow any obstacle to get in between me and the end game. Not even major surgery is enough to persuade me to take a day off.

In 2019, I made the decision to have my 17-year-old breast implants removed. I'd had them done when Corky and I were still together in the futile hope that they would make him find me more attractive and save a marriage which was already on life support.

Well, we all know how *that* story ended.

Years later, at a routine mammogram appointment, the radiographer pointed out that it was almost impossible to see what was going on behind the implant. There could be a tumour or even several of them lurking back there and we might never know until it was too late.

That, understandably, struck the fear of God into me, making me think back to filming my episode of *Who Do You Think You Are?* which traced my family roots and uncovered a story about my maternal great-grandfather dying from multiple tumours aged just 31.

I'd always been told he'd died of a broken heart after his wife had left him, but now I was joining the dots and coming to realise there was a clear history of cancer in the family. As well as my great-grandad, my auntie Mona and auntie Jean had both died of it, then came my mother's diagnosis and suddenly I was looking at a situation with red flags waving all over the shop.

I was always vigilant about checking my breasts for lumps and kept up with my doctor for an annual MOT, but if the implants were preventing a thorough examination then it was possibly all for nothing. My body could be holding onto a deadly secret – the implants I'd had put in to try to boost my confidence could be concealing something that was killing me.

My mum told me to get them removed – she'd never approved of me having them done in the first place because she knew surgery wasn't the solution to my self-esteem issues or a magic pill for my doomed second marriage.

I knew she was right (as per) and spent the next few months conducting a load of my own research around implants and cancer. None of what I found was good. While there was no increased risk of developing the disease from the implants themselves, just as the radiographer had told me, they can make it harder to detect and delayed diagnosis can have terrible consequences.

On top of this, I'd been experiencing a lot of fatigue and general unwellness, almost as if my immune system wasn't quite keeping pace, and a friend of mine suggested those symptoms might be down to the implants.

There is still a lot of ongoing research around all of this, but plenty of good evidence points towards breast implant illness as being a real thing and with the same indicators I'd been experiencing over a number of years.

That was enough for me, I knew what I had to do. I made an appointment with a specialist in Liverpool who referred me to the consultant plastic surgeon Norman Waterhouse at his private clinic in London's Marylebone.

I just wanted rid. By now it was 2019 and we were fast approaching what would be my third series of *Strictly*, but I had convinced myself that these things were slowly killing me and the quicker they were removed the better.

Dr Waterhouse offered to delay the surgery until after the *Strictly* final in December to allow me the time off work to recover, but that wasn't an option for me. I wanted it done yesterday.

I always like to prove to myself that I'm stronger than other people believe, so when the doctors said I needed six weeks, I thought, 'Sod that.'

I was determined not to take any time off at all – the four-hour operation was set for Tuesday 29 October, which, I calculated, would give me four days of rest and recuperation before I was back live on air on the Saturday night.

It was an audacious plan and fraught with jeopardy, but I knew there was only one person who could get me back up and running in that time – my mother. These were the days before she moved in permanently, so she travelled down from Wallasey to stay with me in London when I came home from hospital and I told her I didn't want to hear that I needed to 'rest'.

Her job was to administer an Audrey-style kick up the backside and she swung into action doing what she does best when she's on a mission. She'd get me up out of bed, feed me nutritious soups, make sure I was hydrated and – most importantly – refused to entertain any whining.

My breasts were extremely tender and heavily bandaged with little drains in them to get shot of any excess fluid, but I was surviving only on paracetamol and ibuprofen for the pain and inflammation. I'd refused the morphine as I wanted to be focused and alert on Saturday night with no risk of slurred words.

After four days of turbo-charged recovery, I can't say I felt ready to take on the world, but I was standing, *compos mentis*, and determined. As I climbed into the car waiting to take me to the studio on that Saturday, I winced with the pain and turned to look at my mum, the tears pricking in my eyes.

She gave me short shrift.

'You can wipe those away, girl,' she said, 'Going back to judge today was your choice so take a painkiller and off you go. You can do this.'

That was the job I'd asked her to do, after all.

My *Strictly* family did everything in their power to keep me comfortable – Motsi gave me the gentlest of hugs while my glam squad worked their magic – Alexandria Reid, my stylist, had found a beautiful dinner suit with a white shirt which was super stylish but looser fitting and kinder to wear than my usual structured gowns.

I heard my mum's voice in my head telling me I could do this. And I did.

Not because anyone expected me to – I did it for me. It's only me who I'm competitive with and I've been this way since I was a small girl. For instance, I can't cook for toffee and openly admit to that – it's a running joke in my family – but when I did ITV's *Cooking with the Stars* in 2021, I was so hungry to win I even surprised myself.

The show teams eight celebrities up with a professional chef as a mentor (like a culinary version of *Strictly*) and then contestants go head-to-head preparing a range of dishes. My butter-poached chicken and Keralan-spiced chicken thighs saw me sail through to week four when my lacklustre sole meunière plonked me into the cook-off with McFly's Harry Judd.

Sadly, my chocolate soufflé lost out to Harry's superior version of the dessert and he was the eventual winner of the whole series so there was no shame in losing out to him, but that competitive streak had come out in all its force.

I have no idea where it originates, it doesn't run in the genes, there's no one else like me in the family – I'm a mystery to my own mother, who is still trying to work me out.

My brother had a touch of that mindset, though. If he was lifting weights, he had to lift the heaviest load; if we were racing each other along the beach, he had to win; if he lost a board game he would go off in a sulk.

The big difference between us was that David found it difficult to stick at something in the same way I did. I used my setbacks as a motivation rather than allowing them to get inside my head, torture me and convince me that it was all impossible.

It's a bit like standing at the edge of a dark forest full of brambles. You can't see the other side, but you know you've got to reach it somehow and find a way through the hazards and the unknown.

I have always carried on through the forest.

Some see that as a flaw, this refusal to capitulate even when the odds are stacked against me, but it's healthy for me because that's the way I'm built.

The day I give in I might as well just pour myself a cocoa, read a book and be done.

'If you talk about it, it's a dream, if you envision it, it's possible, but if you schedule it, it's real.'

TONY ROBBINS

One of my all-time favourite songs is Frank Sinatra's iconic 'My Way'. Calling it a song doesn't really do it justice because it's so much more than that, it's a powerful statement from someone who is acknowledging they didn't always get it right, but gave life everything they had, regardless.

I travelled each and every highway …
I did it my way.

Those lyrics resonate with me more than I can describe.

If I want to be the choreographer of my own life and live it on my terms, that means trusting my compass and doing what I believe to be the 'right thing', irrespective of whose ego it pricks. Dance isn't just what I do, it's who I am, so I will stop at nothing to protect it.

The British Open to the World championships used to be the biggest and most prestigious competition in the world, but due to everyone falling out with each other, the whole set-up has been dysfunctional for many years.

Those of us who have no interest in the fighting are trying to get Blackpool back up where it belongs and to a standard of competition that's neutral, transparent and fair. That's why I accepted an offer and chose to go back in May 2025 to judge for the first time in several years, and I know some were upset about that decision – there were a few ripples of disquiet when I announced it.

I thought about it long and hard and it was completely my own decision. The reason I made that choice was because if I'm telling our young dancers about the importance of standing up and deciding for themselves, I need to practise what I preach. I'm going to judge anything and everything I choose.

Blackpool will always have a piece of my heart. I love going to the Tower Ballroom with *Strictly* every year because it brings back so many childhood memories. The Winter Gardens, where the championships take place, evokes that same nostalgia and it's a venue I've held many book events at since I embarked on my literary career. So many full-circle moments.

I've also judged the European championships for Sammy, who is co-founder of the World Dance Council Amateur League, and I will also continue to do events for the World Dance Organisation, crossing those divides, because I want to pave the way for others and show the younger generation that I make my own decisions.

I've been to see the American author and motivational speaker Tony Robbins four times and he has given me so many tools to aid independent thought. I used to think that knowledge was power, but it's not. Knowledge is only *potential* power; action is where power lies.

If it doesn't work, by all means change direction, but never give up on something that you're passionate about. Try it, and deal with the consequences, win, lose or draw. It's so important to say you tried rather than living with the what if. Go ahead and worry about 'what if' later.

Do it your way.

Shirley's Shimmers

Learn to say no without guilt or caveat.
It is a complete sentence.

✗

Make your own choices and own them.

✗

Where your focus goes, energy flows.

✗

When you consistently prove yourself,
you put yourself in the driving seat.

✗

Work hard to invest in yourself – you are worth the effort.

✗

Stop comparing yourself to others and instead
only compare yourself to yesterday's you.

✗

Discipline and work ethic will open the door
to greater freedom to be your own boss.

STEP THIRTEEN

Face the Music

FEARLESSNESS

'Never let yourself
be defeated.'

AUDREY

*A*pparently, the phrase 'face the music' dates all the way back to nineteenth-century theatre and the moment an actor would step onto the stage and turn towards the orchestra pit.

This was their time to shine – the point of no return – and it was make or break.

There's another theory that it originated in the armed forces when a soldier was discharged in dishonour and had to stand before their regiment, often to the sound of a military band.

Either way, it's come to symbolise something much more universal and became immortalised in the classic song by Irving Berlin, 'Let's Face the Music and Dance', which many of you will know accompanied one of Fred Astaire and Ginger Rogers's most celebrated routines in the movie *Follow the Fleet*.

The lyrics are a striking metaphor for how we can choose to approach fear.

There may be trouble ahead,
But while there's moonlight,
And music and love and romance,
Let's face the music and dance.

Facing the music is the reckoning. The dance is where the magic starts to happen.

I truly believe that the more you lean into discomfort, the further it diminishes. I know most people will see me as I appear on *Strictly* – all eyelashes and evening dresses – and draw conclusions or assumptions from that.

From the age of 12, it's been glam up, slap your tan on, get your hair done and the more sequins the better.

But there's another side of me, one where I like to step outside of my comfort zone and, well, face the music. I like to get my hands dirty.

Dance is my safety, my shelter, it's where I'm in control and I will always be grateful for what it gives me. However, I'm a big believer in venturing out of that familiarity bubble every once in a while, ditching the security blanket and doing things that scare me. Confronting fears head on instead of running, hiding and pretending they don't exist is what leads to personal growth. It builds confidence, silences that pesky self-doubt and reveals what you're really made of.

For instance, you may be frightened of public speaking, but staring down that fear could mean starting off with a short presentation in front of a small group. Getting over that first hurdle means the next time won't be nearly as terrifying and the anxiety will relinquish some of its control over you.

One of the most daunting experiences I've ever had came when my boss at *Strictly*, Louise Rainbow, asked me to dance the Samba live on my debut show in order to introduce me to the viewers.

My heart dropped like a stone at the mere suggestion. At that time, I was more used to my flat teaching shoes than the

Latin stilettoes and now suddenly, more than 20 years after retirement, I was being asked to perform a Samba – one of the most energetic, electrifying and rhythmically complex dances in all of Latin – to millions of people.

I didn't think I could do it. I worried about my stamina, about forgetting the steps, about tripping up and falling flat on my face, figuratively and literally.

I told Louise about all my doubts and asked if there was any way we could drop the idea and try something else which didn't require me to take centre stage. But she was adamant.

'You've got to trust me on this, Shirley,' she said. 'I need to introduce you to the public so that they can see that you can dance from the off. I don't want you sat behind a desk and have people judge you when they don't know who you are, where you've come from and what you've achieved in your career.'

So, then. Looked like I was Samba-ing.

The idea behind the performance was that the professional ensemble would dance this wonderful, high-energy routine and I'd enter the fray in the middle to Daft Punk's 'Get Lucky', a track which still gives me tingles and which I chose for my *Desert Island Discs* appearance in 2023.

All the other dancers were in white while I was in a bright red Latin dress which had been made especially for me, so there would be no blending into the crowd. This was my moment and I was petrified.

I picked people I'd taught in the past – AJ Pritchard and Kevin Clifton – to dance with as I made my way onto the dance floor so it would feel as reassuring and familiar as possible, but the nerves were in overdrive all day.

However, I knew I had to get out there and shake it, sweaty palms and all, and that's what I did – although my stomach was doing somersaults the whole time. I strode on and Aljaž Škorjanec spun me round and passed me to AJ for a criss-cross Bota Fogo, then it was on to Giovanni for a promenade run, ending up in the arms of Kevin before I sashayed my way across the dance floor, exiting stage right.

'Thank God, that's over,' was my first thought as soon as I was off camera. And then I heard the director call, 'OK, everybody in position for take two!'

WHAT?!

We were doing it all over again, argh! The big dance numbers in *Strictly* are often pre-recorded and then spliced into the live show and so I think we shot four versions in the end to make sure all the camera angles were perfect.

I didn't think my heartbeat was ever going to slow down; it was thumping so hard it felt as though it might punch through my chest. But once I'd had time to calm down and reflect, I was so bloody pleased with myself for smashing through the walls – walls I'd built up entirely on my own. Suddenly I felt invincible. I'd shown myself and everyone watching that I could still get out there and strut my stuff. I could more than hold my own on that dance floor with professional dancers half my age and I found the whole experience incredibly rewarding.

You're never too old to try something bold, hey?

I didn't have a clue how I'd looked and I felt nervous all over again when it came to watching it back, but when I finally plucked up the courage to peek from in between my fingers, I saw that I hadn't done too badly at all. The routine had captured the high-energy vibe of the night and Louise was dead right to have pushed me – it unlocked a whole new level of bravery in me which has led to greater confidence and a version of myself I feel genuinely proud of.

Now, rather than dreading it, I love the mix of nerves and excitement which rush through me each week when us four judges walk out onto the *Strictly* dance floor and we use those 16 beats to meet in the middle, take our bows and accept the applause. Yes, I still get the collywobbles, but I embrace the moment and bask in the adoration and I'm not embarrassed to say that. It's the same feeling I had when I danced and competed.

I've also started doing the demonstration segments on *It Takes Two* with Kai Widdrington, showing off a bit of Paso here, a spot of Tango there, and it gets me out there and dancing even at the grand old age of 65. I'm the one taking the lead and presenting those pieces to camera, which is not something I'd ever have pictured myself doing.

What a turnaround. It didn't take a miracle to get me there. It just needed a little bit of pluck and that first step of the Samba to crack the whole thing open.

'We gain strength, and courage, and confidence by each experience in which we really stop to look fear in the face ... we must do that which we think we cannot.'

ELEANOR ROOSEVELT

The thing about facing your fears is that one minute you're looking for a new challenge and the next you're 200 feet off the ground on a partially broken suspension bridge across a 200-foot-wide Costa Rican canyon.

My mother never wanted me to accept the *Celebrity Bear Hunt* job and she didn't speak to me for a week after I signed up. She was so worried about me contracting malaria or getting bitten by a snake. Or plummeting 200 feet down a canyon to a certain and grisly death.

'I've lost one child, I don't want to lose another,' she said. 'You're too old, you're going to hurt yourself.'

But I wanted to test and push myself and conquer some of my fears, which is how I ended up on the Bridge the Gap challenge, a high-stakes trial of balance, courage, psychological endurance and teamwork.

Each team had to transport ten supply bags across the ravine using a winch system, while simultaneously replacing the missing slats in the bridge to enable us to walk over it. We were given three loose planks to fill those gaps but only two team members were allowed on the bridge at any time, which meant we had to work out a system to pass the wood down the line in order for us all to get across.

The slightest foot out of place would mean a fall, which, you could argue, is a pretty drastic way to confront my fear of heights, but you know that I tend not to do things by halves. Whichever one of the two teams completed the task in the quickest time would win the challenge and be saved from being sent to the Bear Pit.

I was on a team with Danny Cipriani and Una Healy who couldn't have been more supportive, but we were at a huge disadvantage from the off as we had to go first, meaning we didn't get a chance to strategise. We were presented with the challenge and had to step to it immediately, whereas the red team were able to get into a huddle for 20 minutes and work out a game plan.

I'll make no bones about it, I was absolutely terrified up there. Obviously we were all harnessed to the hilt, but it felt like life or death and there was a moment where I was standing right in the middle of the bridge and had to physically turn around to face the other way to take the slat from Danny and the fear was so strong I could taste it.

But the only way through was to stay focused and, if you watched it, you'll have seen that I didn't shout, yelp or scream or perform any of the histrionics I know make good telly. When I'm in the zone, I go quiet. I have to stay inside myself, form an outer shell and zero in, because quitting this challenge was not an option.

I knew Danny was nervous for me and the task ceased to be about winning and all about the three of us making it across to the other side safely and in one piece. For a guy like Danny who played top-level rugby union for 20 years, represented England and has been trained to win since he was a young boy, he had an extraordinary amount of compassion and it was heartening to see that chivalry still exists. He made me believe that there are still good men out there who give a damn, because I had been starting to wonder.

During my time on the show, I always wanted to be on Danny's team because I knew he would be kind. Kindness is not something I'm used to in my day job, but he has been raised well and is a grounded, all-round brilliant guy. I'll never forget that.

We lost Bridge the Gap by some margin, but I felt I'd achieved something far greater in squaring up to my fear of heights – Bear Grylls recognised that too when he saved me from being sent to the Pit, despite my slow and steady approach probably being the main reason we lost.

Bear compared me to a 'multi-million-dollar racehorse' and said he believed I had significant potential in the contest overall. I was overcome in that moment and although I tried to hold them back, there was nothing I could do to stop the tears.

Danny and Una would have been justified in feeling slightly aggrieved that I'd dodged the Pit, but they were both so lovely to me which made me even more emotional! I was lucky to find myself with a bunch of fellow contestants who were such wonderful human beings.

I felt a motherly love towards Lottie Moss, and I got on especially well with Steph McGovern whom I knew before we went in. She's a superstar.

And then there was Boris Becker whom I absolutely fell in love with. You know when you meet people and feel an instant connection? With Boris I felt that.

'Where has this man been all my life?' I thought. LOL!

I'd followed his career and knew what he'd achieved in tennis, including that unforgettable 1985 Wimbledon victory aged just 17. He's one of the all-time greats and his sporting prowess speaks for itself.

But what I really liked about Boris was his humanity and openness when it came to sharing his life. He'd sit there and tell his amazing stories in such a calm, quiet, soothing way; he was very kind, so observant and helpful to the younger people. He just had a wonderful aura about him and I guess as the two older contestants, we were Mum and Dad of the camp. I learned so much listening to him and was fascinated by the fact he wasn't afraid to talk about having been in prison for bankruptcy fraud, an experience for him where he lost everything and had to start his life all over again.

How impressive that he was able to talk about it with such humility. How generous of him. I like interesting people with interesting stories and admire it when they can talk about those experiences because vulnerability leads to connection and creates a space for the rest of us to learn.

Sadly, Boris injured his ankle and had to leave the show before he took part in any of the challenges but while he was in the camp, he was the best company. He's written me the most lovely messages since the show was filmed and I know we will stay in touch, but my word did he leave a huge gap in the group. I only ever wanted the camp to run smoothly but once we lost Boris, it felt as if I was going at the challenge alone.

I know there's this perception that the basic living arrangements on these shows are all for the cameras and what actually happens is we're ferried off to a luxury hotel when filming finishes for the day.

Scout's honour, we were eating, sleeping and washing in that jungle hut and there was no respite. The beds were tiny; Big Zuu sat on his and it promptly broke in half. We were all sleeping in the same space. Some people snored, some didn't put their things away so there was mess all over the floor.

Then there were the bloody spiders, I've never seen any so big and they definitely hadn't warned me about them before I went in. Probably for the best because had I known, I may not have made it out of Heathrow.

We had mosquito nets over the beds, but all manner of critters and bugs still managed to crawl in and I couldn't get used to that. There were things I didn't want to visualise scuttling across the floor all night – you could hear them click-click-clicking and I would lie there praying that they wouldn't manage to creep up the side of my bed.

You might have gathered that I'm not a jungle person and I'm no spring chicken either, but nevertheless, I threw everything at it, even volunteering to drink Bear's pee when he demonstrated a survival tactic for staying hydrated.

The physical and mental challenges were equally tough and a lot of it scared me stiff, but the only thing I didn't want to happen was to be sent home first. I wouldn't have minded second, I just didn't want to be the first.

I dug in, made all the beds, cleaned all the dishes. I was sous chef to Big Zuu, helped take care of people's emotions and became a bit of a mother. I told everyone at the start of the camp that I was somebody who likes to keep moving – I'll make you a coffee, not because I want the brownie points, but because I'm the sort of person who can't sit still. For me it was a privilege to help keep that place immaculate because that's just what I like to do and everyone was so gracious to let me do that.

In the end I made it to episode seven after being hunted down and caught in the Bear Pit, a pursuit which admittedly left me very shaken. But I was delighted to have got that far. I think Mum, despite her misgivings, was proud of me too.

People go on about these shows being 'life-changing' and bang on about the 'journey' they've been on. At my age, it was never going to be life-changing and it would be wrong of me to claim it was. It's just another interesting part of the puzzle, a chapter in my story and an enriching experience I will remember forever.

That's why I'm always saying to people, take the opportunities, say yes to the challenges because you don't know who you're going to meet or what you're going to take away from them.

All those *Bear Hunt* contestants brought something unexpected to me. As well as Boris, I check in on Lottie from time to time, Kola Bokinni came to a party at my house, Danny always sends me little messages and Steph and I have become quite close, too.

How wonderful that even at my age, I get to welcome new people into my life who enhance it in even small ways?

I proved a lot to myself on that show, most of all that I *can* be OK on my own. I would often go and sit by the sea alone and I found those moments to be meaningful and reflective. I also learned that I'm able to survive without a mobile phone – the producers took those from us at the beginning and it was the best detox I've ever had.

I'm glad I ignored my mum and my friends who were urging me to turn the job down. I'm glad I listened to the inner child who was urging me to 'have a go' and not the older, more cautious woman inside who was saying, 'Nah, don't do this, Shirley. Everyone else is going to be much younger and it's going to be way too far out of your comfort zone.'

These two personas often clash. The child in me recognises that I spent my teenage years dancing, so this is now my time and the chance to live a little. She tells me to go for it.

But there's always Wary Wilma over here saying, 'Don't do that, you're way too old.'

When she starts getting too loud, I shut her up. She doesn't run my show.

> *'Obstacles are like wild animals. They are cowards but they will bluff you if they can. If they see you're afraid of them, they're liable to spring upon you. But if you look them squarely in the eye, they will slink out of sight.'*

ORISON SWETT MARDEN

If you want to shine a light on a cause you believe in, you have to be prepared to do something that stops people in their tracks.

You want the public to sit up and pay attention and – most importantly – donate. So when I had a meeting in 2023 with CALM and we were bandying around fundraising ideas, I knew we were going to have to think big in order to get the pick-up. Having me baking a load of cookies and selling them off simply wasn't going to cut the mustard.

Call me stark raving mad, but that's how we landed on the plan of a triple challenge over three death-defying days, the first of which would see me take on the fastest zipline in the world, soaring for the best part of a mile over Penrhyn Quarry. Day two would be a wing walk where I'd be flying at 110 miles per hour while strapped to the rig of an aeroplane.

The third day would see me jumping out of a plane at 13,000 feet for a skydive.

As you do.

I knew that the more I pushed myself, the more I'd raise for the charity and the further I'd spread the message about mental health awareness and suicide. If my exploits managed to save even one life then they had all been worthwhile.

I kept telling myself that this was for David and all the other lost souls just like him.

And besides all the benefits for the charity, for me personally it would be something else ticked off the bucket list and a chance to test my limits, which is where I thrive.

The plane jump was by far the most terrifying and I'm afraid my focused 'stay in the zone' façade failed miserably that day – I screamed blue murder. But it was exhilarating and life-affirming and when I hit the ground I was lost for words and full of emotion.

David was with me that day.

And there have been so many moments over the years where I've felt him driving me on. There was the celebrity trek up Kilimanjaro in 2018 in aid of Comic Relief, which was ridiculously punishing – the altitude plays havoc with your mind, your ears are popping and it's difficult to breathe – but I believed David was there.

I could even hear him rustling around me when things got particularly treacherous and we were climbing the snowy side of the mountain overnight on the last leg to get to the peak.

When I was asked to take part in that challenge, I was still very new to TV, so I felt honoured to have been approached.

My son said, 'Do you even know where Kilimanjaro is?'

'No idea,' I said.

So we looked it up together.

'You're going to the top of that, Mum. You're absolutely bonkers.'

Maybe I was! Quite apart from the climb, the sleeping arrangements made me baulk because we were in these small tents with no facilities and it was flipping freezing. I hate camping. I hadn't camped in nearly 50 years and each of us had to pitch our own tents, which I didn't have a Scooby how to do. I also couldn't bear the thought of going without a wash – it made me shudder because I can't do grubby. But as I knew from childhood, you just need to find a way round it.

So, I took a couple of the tin bowls we had and used my allocation of water to give myself a good wash – including my hair – and I taught the Little Mix girls, Jade Thirlwall and Leigh-Anne Pinnock, how to do it, too. When you've spent time as a kid bathing in the sink, often without hot water, then washing your hair in a bowl is no big deal. I'd be frozen in my tent and washing in the nuddy, but even if I'd had to stand outside and do it naked in front of 5,000 people I'd have been OK with that, as long as I could be clean.

Before the trip I had been worried that being the oldest, I'd struggle with the physical challenge of the trek. But I'd underestimated how fit a lifetime of dance makes you and I was at the front of the pack throughout until producers told me on the last day that I needed to hang back so that we all made it to the summit as a group.

Having said that, there were many points where I thought I wasn't going to make it. Walking for miles in the heat and high altitude carrying a heavy backpack and your own water supply is a brutal test of character and resolve.

But I knew it was mind over matter, so I had to shut that noise out and keep moving, walking through my deepest fears and silencing my doubts, knowing that it all came down to me.

Same as it ever was.

We are all capable of so much more than we realise – it's the head that puts the blockers on and stops us.

'Take a leap of faith. You will either land somewhere new or learn to fly.'

ANONYMOUS

If, a few years ago, someone had told me that I'd be up on a stage singing 'Boom, Boom, Boom, Boom!!' by the Vengaboys for a TV audience of millions while dressed as a rat in a pair of dungarees, I'd have said they were likely certifiable.

But here we are. Welcome to my life.

When producers of *The Masked Singer* called and asked if I wanted to take part in the new series which would air in January 2024, nobody – and I mean nobody, not even Mark – wanted me to do it. Mainly because I can't sing to save my life – or so I've been told.

But there was that inner child again telling me to do it. Do it, do it! And she won again. Yesterday is gone, tomorrow is promised to nobody, we only have now, so let's live for that.

My thought process was that it would be interesting to have an experience where I maybe felt some of what our *Strictly* celebs go through on that dance floor. I was eager to know what they might feel when they come down the famous staircase ready to put on the biggest performance of their life and what it was like for somebody who had never danced a step going out in front of people who are going to judge them. I'd never had a singing lesson, so there would be parallels.

If you've not seen *The Masker Singer*, the show has a load of celebrities each performing a song while wearing elaborate head-to-toe costumes to conceal their identities. The studio audience and a panel of judges have to try and guess who's in the costume based on clues given throughout the show as well as the celebrity's voice and mannerisms.

At the end of each episode, the singer with the fewest votes is eliminated and has to remove their mask to reveal who they are.

The whole things operates in the strictest of secrecy, it's all very cloak and dagger to make sure your identity isn't leaked, so I couldn't share what I was up to outside of my immediate circle.

I went over to the US and, with his earplugs in, my son attempted to help me with holding a tune. He did his best, bless him.

One thing I was certain about was the costume I wanted to wear. I helped the team design 'Ratty' as a little nod to an incident years ago when a lady at the top of the dance industry bought me a birthday gift, a book called *The Year of the Rat*. No prizes for subtlety there.

The same woman also bought me a crown one year 'because you think you're the queen' long before I actually became known as the Queen of Latin. I still have that crown; those kinds of slights only galvanise me.

On the days we were filming at ITV, it was a military operation to make sure no one saw me out of costume. I was escorted to my dressing room on my own floor in silence wearing a mask and gloves and was only allowed to remove them once I was safely inside.

There's someone designated to hold your hand to guide you through the studio corridors, but you're not to speak to them. This tickled me because one of the dancers from the *Strictly* tour, Jake Leigh, also works on *The Masked Singer*, and he was my hand holder – I was so worried he'd catch on and my cover would be blown but he didn't have a clue it was me!

I enjoyed every minute of it, even singing live on stage inside that claustrophobic costume and I think I did rather well. I got as far as episode three, belting out a passable rendition of 'Nelly the Elephant', before the studio audience put me in the danger zone, but the panel of Davina McCall, Jonathan Ross, Olly Murs and Mo Gilligan didn't guess who I was and they were all shocked when I revealed myself. Job done.

My biggest claim from the series is that I beat pop and soul legend Dionne Warwick – she went out first, would you believe?

I gave it a good go. Life doesn't wait, it passes when we blink, so why not indulge in anything and everything that comes our way while we can? When I get to the place God's intending for me, I don't want to say I didn't do it, I should have done it, why didn't I try it.

And I certainly don't want to say it was because I was too scared.

One day, perhaps in the not-too-distant future, I'd like to do *I'm a Celebrity … Get Me Out of Here!* Snakes, spiders, confined spaces, being trapped somewhere I can't leave – all fears I'd like to conquer. I don't like the dark and still sleep with the light on and I'd quite like to figure out the reason why and hopefully find a little bit more out about myself that way.

There are so many things I still want to try. I've travelled all over the world but seen virtually none of it because I was always dancing, so I'd like to explore places like Brazil and Argentina and, who knows, maybe I'll be brave enough to do that alone.

I've proved that I can step into the unknown – I'm not fearless, I'm just no longer afraid of fear.

Big difference.

Shirley's Shimmers

Every time you face a new fear, you learn
what you're capable of and start to build resilience.

✗

You'll never know how strong you are until you
challenge yourself – comfort is the enemy of progress.

✗

Courage can become a habit.

✗

Feel the fear and do it anyway – growth begins
where your comfort zone ends.

✗

Fear is only as deep as the mind allows it to be –
confront it and its power dissipates.

✗

You haven't come this far to only come
this far … keep going.

STEP FOURTEEN

Keep Dancing

PERSEVERANCE

'Life can be summed up in three words: it goes on.'

AUDREY

*I*t's probably the most famous sign-off in British television. When that fabulous pair of powerhouses Tess Daly MBE and Claudia Winkleman MBE close *Strictly Come Dancing* with the instruction to 'Keeeeeeep dancing!', it's a feelgood sparkly end to a Saturday night well spent.

But it can also be a mantra for life. Heartbreak, grief, burn-out, doubt – all of them and more besides can cause us to falter. But if we step up even when our hearts are heavy, if we're able to persevere and persist, to keep going, keep moving and keep living, we can find the slivers of light.

We can find rhythm in the chaos.

I'm known as a survivor in my industry – remember the quote I shared with you right at the beginning of this book about however many times people try to put me down, I always seem to pop up somewhere else? That's the truth. What the mind can conceive, it can achieve and even if all the doors are closed shut, I'll find a crack somewhere and prise one open.

There have been more downs than ups, trust me, and my life never seems to be on an even keel. Who knows, maybe the even keel would be boring.

But I've learned to cherish the ups because they can be so few and far between. I savour them, soak them in. When it comes to the downs, there's no choice but to face and deal with them. Power through because this too will pass.

But it's about moving anyway and not allowing those worst of times to define you. It's refusing to stay stuck and knowing that even the smallest of steps forward is a stitch in the wound.

I will not go down without a fight. I'll grit my teeth, put those gloves on and stand up for myself. It's an instinct learned from a housing estate where you had to know how to scrap and when to leg it for your life.

There's a little flicker inside of me, burning quietly. As long as there is breath in my body, it won't ever go out.

'You don't have a right to the cards you believe you should have been dealt. You have an obligation to play the hell out of the ones you're holding.'

CHERYL STRAYED

Going back to teach after David died was the hardest thing I've ever done and I had to draw on every reserve I had – every bit of the strength of character I'd built over a lifetime – to get through it.

We lost him in December and I returned to the studio early in the new year, not knowing if it was the 'right' time and not wanting to leave my mother either. What I did know was that I had to get back at some point and when you're self-employed, there's a bit more pressure.

From January we're always running up to the United Kingdom championships so there would be a lot to keep me busy and my mind occupied although I was existing in this fog of grief.

I only thought about getting to the end of the day. I played the music extra loud and kept moving and found that not only was I able to carry on teaching, but for the time I was in the studio, I was able to forget about the profound trauma we were dealing with on the outside. I'd walk in there and for a few sacred hours I'd feel some light relief.

Hang your problems at the door, as my mother would say. Pick them up on your way out.

Having that structure and normality to my day gave me stability and purpose. I wasn't denying or ignoring my grief, but I was starting to build a framework in which I could begin to heal.

Dance has been my saviour in so many ways throughout my life. I'm so lucky that I can go to work, put on the music, teach my couple and get lost in a space that looks after me. Working and teaching is my haven.

Dance still makes the hairs on the back of my neck stand on end. Whether I'm watching a performance or dancing a routine myself, I can get lost in a world of my own, just me and the music and movement in the body.

But it's not a lasting feeling and you're only lighter while you're in it. It's not like a piece of art on the wall you can sit and admire for a while and return the next day for the same experience. My industry is about the feeling right there in the here and now, one which you'll never recapture.

People often say, 'Oh, it felt so good yesterday when I was dancing, and not so much today.' The look of the dance will be the same, but it's the feeling that's changed. We all have this sensory zone inside our body, this kinetic connection with ourselves, and my relief from various troubles comes in the moment. But I can't hold on to it, I can't grasp it. I can't put it in a basket and keep it.

It's a momentary escape, but an escape nonetheless.

> *'I can be changed by what happens to me. But I refuse to be reduced by it.'*
>
> MAYA ANGELOU

If there's anyone who knows just how to 'keep dancing', it's *Strictly* professional Amy Dowden. I taught her when she was a young girl and she's always been a gorgeous dancer. She's a great teacher too, but even more than that, she's a wonderful human being and brings something very special with her wherever she goes.

Amy was diagnosed with stage three breast cancer in May 2023 after discovering a lump in her right breast on her honeymoon. Within weeks she was undergoing a mastectomy before starting a course of chemotherapy, which she bravely detailed for a BBC documentary – they started filming just six days after her diagnosis, she was so determined to raise awareness and record every moment, no matter how raw.

Her treatment ruled her out of that year's *Strictly*, something I know she was devastated by, but she was bullish about returning to the dance floor and, sure enough, she made a surprise appearance in the group finale that December, a moment which moved the nation.

Everyone was thrilled when it was announced she was to come back in September 2024 with a celebrity partner, having been given the all-clear from cancer, and it wasn't long before she was dazzling audiences again with her performances in the arms of JB Gill. What a story of triumph over tragedy and of hope over despair.

Sadly, Amy's run on the series was cut short after she sustained an injury in training. But, thank goodness, she was able to join us on the nationwide tour in January 2025 and that was the mark of a true champ.

She kept dancing and then some.

I've been in the room with Amy when she's sobbed her heart out. I know how much this terrible illness has taken from her and yet she's still shining bright with that big, beautiful smile of hers.

She has health battles to contend with besides cancer and has been open about her Crohn's disease and the impact it has had on her since childhood. She has had to manage chronic pain and debilitating flare-ups all while navigating a dance career which saw her and her partner Ben Jones crowned British Open Latin Dance champions in 2017.

I think I was one of the first people to encourage her to talk about those difficulties and she went on to make a beautiful documentary, *Strictly Amy: Crohn's and Me*, which my niece Mary, a fellow Crohn's sufferer, also took part in. A remarkable pair of women I'm so proud to have in my life.

Facing down an illness and withstanding everything it throws at you is one thing, but it takes an exceptional kind of strength and generosity to speak publicly about it and share something so personal.

Amy has been selfless and inspirational with the work she's done – all while struggling herself – to uplift and help other women feel comfortable talking about their own journeys. I have such huge admiration for her and I've no doubt that she has saved countless lives with her tireless efforts.

What a role model.

She has endured unimaginable adversity for someone so young but she's never given up on her dreams and she's risen from the trenches with grace, grit and strength. Amy Dowden has danced through her pain and her courageous story is a vivid reminder to us all to live fully, love deeply and never to underestimate the power of hope.

'When you get into a tight place and everything goes against you, till it seems as though you could not hang on a minute longer, never give up then, for that is just the place and time that the tide will turn.'

HARRIET BEECHER STOWE

I'm always aspiring to be a better person but I'm by no means the finished article. Even if I live to 150 I don't think I'll ever be that!

But I do recognise my weak spots and will continue to work on them because I know it takes courage to look inward and acknowledge the parts of myself that may be holding me back or affecting those around me. Aiming to be the best version of me means never hiding or shying away from uncomfortable truths and I reckon I know myself very well by now – flaws and all.

Let's lay it on the line. I can be short tempered and fully admit there are occasions where I throw my toys out the pram if people don't slot into my lane. I treat people as I would wish to be treated myself, but I do have a bristly side and if someone has a go at me, I can get my claws out. Like the day I punched the lights out of the woman who was sleeping with my husband when she drunkenly sidled up to me at the British National Dance Championships and said we 'needed to talk'.

What she and Corky had done had hurt me beyond measure and I had nothing to say to her, but she wouldn't let it go. It was when she said, 'You've just got to get over the fact I fucked your husband' that something in me snapped and, to be frank, I knocked her block off.

There was a stunned silence as I turned on my heel and left – I could hear the whispers, 'Is that Shirley Ballas? Did she just whack that woman?' but I just kept on walking, head high.

When I look back, I should have probably carried myself with a little more decorum – I had a devil on one shoulder and an angel on the other and on this occasion, the devil won. I was immediately horrified by what I'd done, but she'd provoked me on several levels and flicked a switch. It wasn't just the betrayal I was bruised by, but the humiliation too, of thinking that everyone else knew what was going on behind my back. All of those emotions surged to the surface that day and I lashed out. I'm not proud of it.

These days I'm more discerning about my battles – I have to decide what to let go and what to fly at – but being bullied or seeing other people victimised is not something I'll ever put up with again. I've got things wrong, I've misjudged, made bad calls and I've failed. But equally, I'm committed to improvement, learning from those mistakes, getting up and making amends.

I'm philosophical about a lot of the missteps I've made – age and the passage of time bring with them a softness and the sting of mistakes from a lifetime ago fades somewhat. All those questionable choices are things that I've grown and evolved from and I can step back and see the bigger picture now. The past is the past and the present can be so very healing.

When Sammy and I took our British Open the World title in 1983 – the pinnacle of our career – I was in turmoil over my affair with Corky and that cast a shadow over what should have been the happiest moment of my life so far. And my marriage to Corky was on the rocks when we won the same title together in 1995 and 1996. This was the dance equivalent to winning an Olympic gold medal and our son was there in the audience excitedly waving his mum and dad on, but I just felt so lost and empty inside.

It wasn't until I watched Mark win the Mirrorball trophy for the first time on *Dancing with the Stars* in 2008 that I got to experience the pure, unadulterated high I should have had all those years ago. I was the person who gave birth to him, who taught him to dance, who let him fly the nest and who supported him, and when I saw him lift that trophy (and twice more again in subsequent series), I was euphoric and felt the past finally release some of its grip on me.

I also find it fascinating that other people's lives would have looked very different if I hadn't left. Sammy and I were in such a secure position, we were so young and would have gone on to reign for a long time. But once I was out of the picture, Donnie Burns became the world champion with his partner Gaynor Fairweather and Barbara McColl got the partnership of a lifetime with Sammy. By departing the scene, I altered other people's destinies, not just my own.

And what if I *had* stayed married to Sammy? Well, Mark wouldn't be here and the best thing that ever happened to me was giving birth to my son. I have managed to cope with everything else because of him, my biggest joy and greatest achievement, whether he's making me laugh or telling me off. I secretly love getting told off by my son.

I'm blessed that he has a wonderful wife, I couldn't have wished for someone more perfect for him – all you want for your kids is that they'll find someone who makes them happy. BC is that person. I'm also fortunate to still have my mother around – I will always make sure she is taken care of, she deserves that.

My life is complex. I'm not a straightforward, straight-down-the-factory-belt type of person and I know not everybody understands me. But knowing that I'm surrounded by my tight circle of trust gives me the confidence to keep chugging away.

Some people – friends of mine included – are content to stay where they are. They reach a point at which they're happy with what they have and decide to sit back, drink their cocoa and take the slow lane.

Fair play to them. Part of me is in awe of their ability to wind down and pop their feet up, but that's just not me. I feel like there's still so much more to do and I'm always conscious of the fact that once it's over, that's your lot, which is why I try to pack as much into each day as possible.

You never know when it will be your last.

A dear friend of mine, Andrew Sinkinson, king of the Foxtrot, recently passed away at the age of 60 doing what he loved – teaching dance. He died as he lived, in his dancing shoes, and his sudden loss was a shock to our industry as well as a stark reminder of how vanishingly short life is.

So I won't slow down or melt away, not while I still have dreams to chase and a flame in my soul.

And I will keep dancing – in joy and celebration, through sorrow and tears, and always with hope in my heart, until the music finally stops.

I hope you will too.

Shirley's Shimmers

Staying present and keeping at it doesn't mean always having to pretend everything is OK. It just means that you shouldn't allow the bad times to define you or your future.

✖

The rain will fall, but it won't last forever and it will pass quicker if you can keep moving, one step at a time.

✖

Cling on to the glimmers – there are always glimmers – and focus on them during the darker moments.

✖

Showing up consistently and doing the work isn't just about surviving, it's about building self-esteem and eliminating self-doubt.

✖

When life is tough and unpredictable, continuing to engage can give you back a sense of control.

A letter to my 17-Year-Old Self

Dear Shirley,

I've been thinking about you a lot lately. I might have a few more wrinkles these days and a heart that's been crushed more times than I care to tell, but I've also got a truckload of perspective and there's some things I'd like to share with you.

Before we go any further, I want to let you know that you're an incredibly brave young lady. I know for a fact you'll be rolling your eyes at that statement and wafting me away.

'Yeah, yeah,' you'll say. 'Whatever.'

But it's the absolute truth, you just won't realise or appreciate it until decades later.

Upping sticks and moving down to London without any money or prospect of a job in order to pursue a dream and make something of yourself takes guts and if you'd been my daughter I would have almost certainly tried to talk you out of such a ballsy plan.

But you're such a hot-headed, strong-willed little thing with a belly full of fire, it would never have worked, would it? Once you set your mind on something, there's no going back and when people tell you that you can't, it only makes you more determined.

That part of you never changes, by the way.

Life up to this point hasn't been easy – you've been swimming upstream since day one so you're already adept at making the seemingly impossible possible. That's why you've barely batted an eyelid at the squalid flat you're currently living in – it's the only one you can afford so you've rolled up your sleeves and got on with it.

'Twas ever thus.

I can tell you that you're going to continue having to do exactly that because what lies ahead is not a bed of roses. Life is going to throw some wild curveballs in your direction and sometimes it will feel like the whole world is against you.

But whenever you get knocked down, you draw on the resilience instilled in you since childhood – that superpower of yours – and you manage to pick yourself up, keeping the faith that there's always a rainbow on the other side. You will learn and grow the most from the toughest times, so trolley on forward because the brighter days will come.

I want to talk to you about this constant struggle with self-esteem, which breaks my heart to think of now. I know you don't like your body and you never feel thin enough. You worry about the mole on your chin (that's part of what makes you unique, by the way) and your 'crooked' nose (ditto) and unfortunately you've chosen to work in an industry where these perceived flaws will be picked on and magnified. Throughout your career people will tell you that you're 'too big' for your dance partners.

Ignore them. Trust me, when you look back at photographs in years to come, you will see how lovely you are. Stop comparing yourself to others – you are young and you are radiant.

And beauty runs far deeper than the skin. When you get to my age you'll realise it's not about having the best clothes, the prettiest face or the bounciest hair. It's what's in your heart and soul that makes you attractive, so try not to criticise yourself too much because you have a strong moral code which remains steadfast and true whatever shadows cross your path – that counts for something.

I know right now you're just doing what you love, enjoying the adventure, and haven't thought about making it to world champion, but I'm telling you that you have both the talent and the drive to make it to the top.

Dance will give you the most extraordinary life and career. It will take you around the world and give you the kinds of opportunities you could never have imagined growing up. It will pick you up and push you along when the chips are down and give you the strength and discipline to survive the blows.

But it will also take you to the brink, emotionally, physically and mentally. You've been raised to be vigilant, but do keep your wits about you and watch out for those who don't have your best interests at heart.

They will try, try and try again to steer you onto the wrong path but resist this and graft like billy-o to create and control your own destiny. You have a mind of your own and a tongue in your head; don't be afraid to use either one.

While I'm dishing out the all-important life advice, stop getting hung up on things that really aren't worth fretting over. Not everything needs to be immaculate all the time. Not every dish needs to be washed, not every surface needs to be wiped down immediately.

Relax. Let it go. Sometimes it's OK to step off the hamster wheel for a while – you can always get back on it again. It's not going anywhere.

You probably want to know how things turn out for you romantically …

I don't want to spoil the story, but what I will say is that it might not work out in quite the way you envisage right now and you're in for a few surprises.

It will be magical and messy and, my God, you will make mistakes. You're human, so don't beat yourself up about decisions you made with your heart and which you believed were right at the time. But whatever happens, something beautiful emerges from the chaos and you will give birth to a son who will be the light of your life and grow up to be the very best of men.

He will make you prouder than you ever thought possible. There will be a beautiful daughter-in-law, too, and a grandson who will complete your family.

I'll not keep you any longer. No doubt there'll be a dance lesson you've got to dash off to (you'll still be dashing about in your sixties, mind), so I'll leave you to get on with that.

But before I sign off, remember this – you will be underestimated, overlooked and sometimes betrayed. But you will never be broken.

Keep swimming, my darling. You'll be OK.

All my love,

Shirley

xxx

A Final Word from My Mother, Audrey

As mother and daughter, me and Shirley have always been close, but we are quite different characters. I'm a very private person and play my cards close to my chest. Shirley is much more public and sometimes I think she tells the world everything.

She's more forgiving than I am, too, and doesn't seem to hold a grudge for long. I think that's probably a good trait of hers but it's the polar opposite of how I am.

Shirley was always very determined as a little girl, always wanting to be busy, to be number one and the leader, and she was involved in everything. She was a force of nature – some might say pushy – and that personality has taken her a long way.

And of course, she had a huge talent for dance. She definitely doesn't get that from me!

I do love sitting with a whisky and a cigarette on a Saturday night and watching her on *Strictly*, although I get nervous, never really knowing what's going to come out of her mouth.

She's made her mistakes in life and I've often seen those mistakes a mile off, long before they happen. I've got her number, you see. She'll ask for my advice and listen but she doesn't necessarily take it, that's all I'll say.

The only thing I can do as her mother is be there to pick up the pieces, give her a bit of sympathy and then get her back on the straight and narrow. That's my job.

I might not have told her very often, but I've always been proud of her, even when she didn't win. I'm proud of her for what she's survived, as well. We've both had a lot of contend with in our lifetimes and she's had to be strong to come through it.

She's a true fighter, one in a million, and I'm proud to call her my daughter.

ACKNOWLEDGEMENTS

Over the years I've been lucky enough to have many kind, hardworking and wonderful people pass through my life, a lot I've already mentioned throughout the pages of this book, but those that are dear to my heart, those that continue to inspire and support me during my own life lessons are forever in my heart, you all know who you are.

Special thanks to:

My Mother, Audrey, you taught me all my life lessons. You guided me through it all, the good, the bad and the ugly. You taught me this too will pass. Just keep moving along the bus.

David, for always being in my heart.

Mark, for being there twenty-four seven for me always and forever, BC Jean and Banksi, you are my world, best daughter-in-law and grandson ever.

Thanks to Jonathan Shalit, Ashley Vallance and Bex Severn, my team at InterTalent for your supportive guidance in showbiz land. Harry Surplus, my PA, for always keeping my TV side of life organised.

Thanks to Jo Bell, for making this book happen, and to the team at Ebury, especially Albert DePetrillo and Izzy Frost, for your courtesy, insight, and vision for this book. PR and marketing, Lucy Brown and Ellenor Jermyn, thanks for all your support along the way.

Beth Neil, gratitude for helping me write my latest life instalment.

To my fans who have supported me over the last 8 years, thank you for buying my books and reading them. Keep putting your best foot forward throughout your own lives.

Hugs and lots of love,

Shirley B

CREDITS

Irving Berlin, 'Let's Face the Music and Dance'
Lyrics: Irving Berlin
Publisher: Universal Music Publishing Group

Frank Sinatra, 'My Way'
English lyrics: Paul Anka
French lyrics: Claude François and Jacques Revaux
Publisher: Universal Music Publishing Group

'There is no passion to be found playing small or in settling for a life that is less than the one you are capable of living.' Nelson Mandela, *Long Walk to Freedom*, 1994

'Develop a passion for learning. If you do, you will never cease to grow.' Anthony J. D'Angelo, *The College Blue Book*, 1995

'Stand up for what is right, even if that means standing alone.' Suzy Kassem, *Rise Up and Salute the Sun*, 2011

'Conflict is inevitable, but combat is optional.' Max Lucado, *He Still Moves Stones*, 1992

'If we don't tell our own stories, we'll never take control of the narrative.' Julie Clark, *The Last Flight*, 2020

'Your body is the piece of the universe you've been given, the place where love and joy and grief happen, so honour it.' Geneen Roth, *Women, Food and God: An Unexpected Path to Almost Everything*, 2009

'Never bend your head. Always hold it high. Look the world straight in the face.' Helen Keller, Associated Press, 30 May 1995

'You are never too old to set another goal or to dream a new dream.' C.S. Lewis, *Letters of C.S Lewis*, W.H. Lewis, 1966

'Sometimes it takes a heartbreak to shake us awake and help us see we are worth so much more than we're settling for.' Mandy Hale, *The Single Woman*, 2013

'You are braver than you believe, stronger than you seem, and smarter than you think.' A.A. Milne, *The House at Pooh Corner*, 1928

'[Menopause] is a time of liberation. It's a time of shedding the shackles of inhibition and of giving a damn.' Davina McCall, *Women's Health*, December 2021

'It only takes one voice, at the right pitch, to start an avalanche.' Dianna Hardy, *Return of the Wolf*, 2014

'Beautiful young people are accidents of nature, but beautiful old people are works of art.' Eleanor Roosevelt

'Mental illness is nothing to be ashamed of, but stigma and bias shame us all.' Bill Clinton, The White House Conference on Mental Health, 1999

'Life is truly known only to those who suffer, lose, endure adversity and stumble from defeat to defeat.' Anaïs Nin, *The Diary of Anaïs Nin*, 1966

'Never get so busy making a living that you forget to make a life.' Dolly Parton. Posted on official Twitter account @DollyParton, 9 August 2010

'Almost everything will work again if you unplug it for a few minutes, including you.' Anne Lamott, *Book by Bird*, 1994

'The bad news is time flies. The good news is you're the pilot.' Michael Altshuler

'The secret of life is to fall seven times and to get up eight.' Paulo Coelho, *The Alchemist*, 1988

'You gain strength, courage, and confidence by every experience in which you really stop to look fear in the face.' Eleanor Roosevelt, *You Learn by Living*, 1960

'Don't waste your energy trying to change opinions. Do your thing, and don't care if they like it.' Tina Fey, *Bossypants*, 2011

'If you talk about it, it's a dream, if you envision it, it's possible, but if you schedule it, it's real.' Tony Robbins, Facebook, May 25 2024

'We gain strength, and courage, and confidence by each experience in which we really stop to look fear in the face … we must do that which we think we cannot.' Eleanor Roosevelt, *You Learn by Living* 1960

'Obstacles are like wild animals. They are cowards but they will bluff you if they can. If they see you're afraid of them, they're liable to spring upon you. But if you look them squarely in the eye, they will slink out of sight.' Orison Swett Marden, *He Can Who Thinks He Can*, 1908

'You don't have a right to the cards you believe you should have been dealt. You have an obligation to play the hell out of the ones you're holding.' Cheryl Strayed, *Tiny Beautiful Things*, 2012

'I can be changed by what happens to me. But I refuse to be reduced by it.' Maya Angelou, *Letter to My Daughter*, 2008

'When you get into a tight place and everything goes against you, till it seems as though you could not hang on a minute longer, never give up then, for that is just the place and time that the tide will turn.' Harriet Beecher Stowe, *Oldtown Folks*, 1869